THE MACMILLAN BOOK OF
EARLIEST CHRISTIAN HYMNS

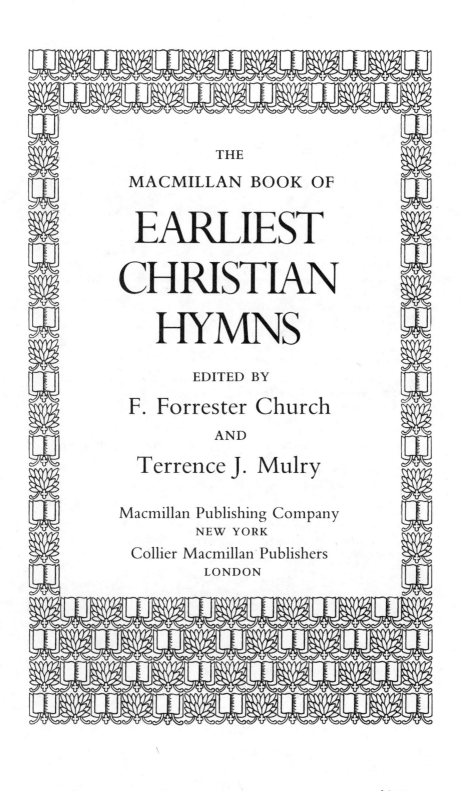

THE

MACMILLAN BOOK OF

EARLIEST CHRISTIAN HYMNS

EDITED BY

F. Forrester Church

AND

Terrence J. Mulry

Macmillan Publishing Company
NEW YORK
Collier Macmillan Publishers
LONDON

Macmillan Publishing Company
866 Third Avenue, New York, NY 10022
Collier Macmillan Canada, Inc.

Library of Congress Cataloging-in-Publication Data

The Macmillan book of earliest Christian hymns/edited by
F. Forrester Church and Terrence J. Mulry.
    p. cm.
  Includes indexes.
  ISBN 0-02-525581-9
  1. Hymns, Early Christian.   I. Church, F. Forrester.   II. Mulry,
Terrence.
BV320.M33 1988
264'.2'09015—dc19   88–15339   CIP

Macmillan books are available at special discounts for bulk purchases for
sales promotions, premiums, fund-raising, or educational use. For details,
contact:

                Special Sales Director
                Macmillan Publishing Company
                866 Third Avenue
                New York, NY 10022

10 9 8 7 6 5 4 3 2 1

Printed in the United States of America

To Holland Hendrix

CONTENTS

Preface   ix

  I. NEW TESTAMENT HYMNS   1

  II. THE ODES OF SOLOMON   29

  III. EARLY HYMNS FROM ORTHODOX
       TRADITIONS   57

  IV. HYMNS FROM THE NEW TESTAMENT
       APOCRYPHA   95

  V. GNOSTIC HYMNS FROM NAG HAMMADI   121

  VI. SAINT EPHREM'S *HARP OF THE SPIRIT*   137

  VII. HYMNS FROM THE EASTERN CHURCH   163

  VIII. THE CRUCIBLE OF LATIN HYMNODY   191

  IX. CLOSING HYMNS: SAINT GREGORY
       THE GREAT   223

Devotional and Topical Index   229
Source and Name Index   231

PREFACE

IF you were to strip worship of all impurities, what would remain? My guess is this: a song. Not a simple song. It would contain many modalities: praise to God, thanksgiving, intercession, and confession—with a poetic recounting of salvation history thrown in for good measure. But one thing is certain: Surely this song would soar beyond the limitations of speech and wing toward heaven, a pure communication between the faithful and all that is holy.

In some ways, this description captures the essence of earliest Christian worship. When Christians first gathered in their new communities to worship God, one of the most important things they did together was sing. An important early document underscores this fact. When asked by the Emperor Trajan in the early second century to investigate any possible crimes Christians might be committing against the Roman state, Pliny, a Roman governor, observing their worship, found no evidence of any crime. Instead, in his report to Trajan, Pliny wrote,

> The sum total of their guilt or error amounted to no more than this, they had met regularly before dawn on a fixed day to chant verses alternately among themselves in honor of Christ as if to a god, and also to bind themselves by oath, not for any criminal purpose, but to abstain from theft, robbery, and adultery, to commit no breach of trust and not to deny a deposit when called upon to restore it. After this ceremony it had been their custom to disperse and reassemble later to take food of an ordinary harmless kind.

This is how it looked from the outside, as recorded by an unsympathetic but impartial observer. From within, it was altogether different. Far from being innocuous, this chanting of verses during worship served to unite an otherwise disparate community in song. Even more important, the songs they sang together imparted a message of salvation to all who sang.

The Macmillan Book of Earliest Christian Hymns is the second volume of three, following *The Macmillan Book of Earliest Christian Prayers* (1988) with *The Macmillan Book of Earliest Christian Meditations* forthcoming. We hope that together these anthologies will provide a comprehensive survey of early Christian devotional literature.

Each collection is designed to facilitate the reader's own personal devotions. Though brief prefaces are offered for each chapter, annotation is kept to a minimum. Translations have been selected more for their literary quality than for their literal fidelity to the original text. And at the end of the book, you will find a devotional index to help locate hymns according to liturgical season and spiritual theme.

In making our selections, we take the word "hymn" to mean what it did nineteen centuries ago, not limiting it to the more narrow modern definition. From your acquaintance with contemporary hymnals, some hymns selected here will instantly be familiar, but we also include canticles, psalms, odes, responsive litanies, and poems. In the ancient sense of the word, a hymn is a song to God. Such songs come in many different guises. Though most of the hymns selected for inclusion here were either sung or chanted during common worship, others were written and published in collections for private devotion. The genre is a broad one, as broad as it is rich.

Hymns were favored in worship for practical as well as aesthetic and theological reasons. Since worship was often performed without written aids, the rhythmic patterns and formulaic repetition that distinguish hymns and chants from readings and prayers served as a mnemonic device for worshipers. Though many of these hymns are longer than those we sing today, the ancient ear was finely tuned, and even lengthy hymns were easily learned by heart.

Christian worship and hymnody are firmly planted in the Jewish liturgical tradition. Initially, the strongest influence upon Christian hymns was the Old Testament Book of Psalms. Together with other songs and canticles contained in the Jewish scriptures, the Psalms offered formal models for communal exaltation and praise. During the first six centuries of the common era, these influences continued, but were supplemented by traditions that even Pliny would have found familiar, including classical poetic forms, and time-honored patterns of imperial worship. From the east, the rhythms and passion of Syriac poetry had an influence as well.

The following collection of earliest Christian hymns permits us to chart the development of Christian worship and hymnody from its vital beginnings to maturity. We have arranged our selections in nine chapters, tracing earliest Christian hymnody from New Testament times to the late sixth century, with Gregory the Great.

Chapter I, "New Testament Hymns," includes a broad selection, ranging from the canticles in Luke, to Pauline hymns, and hymns from the Book of Revelation. Most of the themes, both theological and formal, that emerge during the following centuries, are hinted at here.

Chapter II, "The Odes of Solomon," offers dramatic evidence of the influence of Jewish psalmody upon early Christian hymnody. These hymns, written concurrently with the Gospel of John at the beginning of the second century, might best be described as Christian psalms.

Chapter III, "Early Hymns from Orthodox Traditions," a collection of second- and third-century hymns, testifies to the growing relationship between hymnody and theology. New influences from classical Greek and Roman imperial hymn traditions also appear, supplementing those of Jewish liturgical traditions.

Chapter IV, "Hymns from the New Testament Apocrypha," stems from writings attributed to the apostles, and reflects popular, heterodox, traditions of hymnody. One very unusual hymn, "The Hymn of the Pearl," is the crowning accomplishment of early Christian poetry.

Chapter V, "Gnostic Hymns from Nag Hammadi," gives a wild spin to early Christian hymnody, ecstatic and theologically adventurous. Here, as with certain hymns in the previous chapter, the singer becomes the song.

Chapter VI, "Saint Ephrem's *Harp of the Spirit,*" is a collection of exquisite Syriac hymns from the fourth century. Though little known, perhaps no other early Christian hymn book contains poetry as soaring, all in defense of orthodox teachings.

Chapter VII, "Hymns from the Eastern Church," contains hymns by Saint Basil, Saint John Chrysostom, and Saint Gregory Nazianzus, the finest poet of the Greek Church. Also, with selections from the creeds of Athanasius and Arius, the intimate relationship between Christian hymnody and theology is dramatically underscored.

Chapter VIII, "The Crucible of Latin Hymnody," is a bridge from early Christian to medieval and modern hymnody. The hymns of Saint Hilary, Saint Ambrose, Fortunatus, and Saint Prudentius are models for contemporary hymns, some even enduring to this very day.

Chapter IX, "Closing Hymns: Saint Gregory the Great," provides a brief, telling summation. Almost every theme sounded over the first six centuries of Christian hymnody is touched upon in these four brilliant and moving hymns by one of the great fathers of the church.

As with *The Macmillan Book of Earliest Christian Prayers,* most of the hymns selected here are in the public domain. But we wish to thank the following individuals and publishing houses for permission to republish those that are not: *Early Christian Prayers,* edited by A. Hammon, with an English translation by Walter Mitchell (Chicago: Henry Regnery Company, 1961); *Harp of the Spirit,* edited and translated by Sebastian Grock (London: Fellowship of St. Alban and St. Sergius); *The Nag Hammadi Library in English,* by James M. Robinson et al., editors and translators (New York: Harper and Row, 1977); *New Testament Apocrypha,* Vol. I: Gospel and Related Writings by Edgar Hennecke, edited by Wilhelm Schneemelcher (Tubingen, W.Ger.: Paul Siebeck, 1959), English translation edited by R. McL. Wilson (Cambridge: Lutterworth Press, 1963), published by Westminster Press, Philadelphia; *New Testament Apocrypha,* Vol. II: Related Writings by Edgar Hennecke (Philadelphia: Westminster Press, 1953); *Fathers of the Church,* Vol. 75, edited by Denise Molaise Meehan (Washington, D.C.: Catholic University of American Press); *The Odes of Solomon,* edited and translated by James Hamilton Charlesworth (Oxford: Oxford

University Press, 1973); *Springtime of the Liturgy,* edited and translated by Lucien Deiss, with an English translation by Matthew J. O'Connell (Collegeville, Minn.: The Liturgical Press, Order of St. Benedict, 1979).

We dedicate this collection of hymns to Holland Hendrix, professor of religion at Barnard College. Unbelievably generous in help and advice, Holly saved us from many errors of omission and commission. We take the blame for what may be wrong with this collection, but much that is right here has Holly's stamp on it.

F. Forrester Church

I. New Testament Hymns

When you come together, each one has a hymn

SAINT PAUL (1 COR. 14:26)

I F you read the New Testament with an eye out (or ear open) for hymns, you will discover that it is filled with song. Since the basic elements of early Christian worship were adapted from established and familiar Jewish liturgical patterns, the most direct influence, understandably enough, is the Hebrew scriptures, especially the Psalms. This rich literature, as well as hymnic elements in the Wisdom tradition, was then freely adapted to serve both developing Christian practice (baptismal hymns, for instance) and theology (especially in the Christological hymns and professions of faith).

Our selections begin with the canticles from the first two chapters of Luke: the Magnificat, Benedictus, Gloria, and Nunc Dimittis. All four are reminiscent of Old Testament canticles, especially the songs of Miriam and Moses in Exodus 15. The parallel hymns from Matthew 21 and Mark 11 echo Psalm 118:21, even as the next verse of the same psalm is worked into the prosaic fabric of Mark 12, a clear acknowledgment of source.

Drawing from a different genre of Jewish literature, the Johannine Prologue (The Hymn of John) and Philippians hymn reflect the influence of Wisdom hymns from the Old Testament extracanonical writings (e.g., The Wisdom of Solomon 7:25–8:1, and Ben Sira 1:1–20), which in turn were partly inspired by traditional hymns to Isis (compare Books 10 and 11 in Apuleius's *The Golden Ass*). The Philippian hymn is telling in another way. When he wrote this letter, Paul was engaged in a struggle with the so-called Docetists, Christians who believed that Christ was not fully human and did not suffer. To advance his argument, Paul adapts a Wisdom hymn with "Docetistic" tendencies (suggestions that Christ appeared only in the "likeness of men," merely in human form) by adding the phrase "even the death of the cross" to underscore Christ's suffering and humanity. This is the first indication of how hymns would serve as creative vehicles for polemical or critical theology.

Many of the hymns from the epistles are Christological hymns, spontaneous litanies, rhythmic and patterned professions of faith offered up within the worshiping community in celebration of Christ's triumph and saving work. In addition you will notice doxologies, celebrating the glory of God (such as 1 Peter 4:11), and blessings (such as 1 Peter 1:3–5), forms that found a permanent place as professions of faith in Christian liturgies—the former sung, the latter often chanted. Several hymns included in the epistles, freely woven into prose passages, show up in fragmentary form. We have included reliable reconstructions of two such hymns, restored to their original form by the combination of fragments of the same hymn found in different letters.

This chapter closes with a selection of hymns from the Book of Revelation, a book that Lucien Deiss in *Springtime of the Liturgy* aptly describes as "a vast song of hope." These hymns express that hope eloquently.

My soul doth magnify the Lord,
   and my spirit hath rejoiced in God my Savior.
   For he hath regarded the low estate of his handmaiden:
   for, behold, from henceforth all generations shall call
      me blessed.
   For he that is mighty hath done to me great things;
   and holy is his name.

   And his mercy is on them that fear him from
      generation to generation.
   He hath showed strength with his arm;
   he hath scattered the proud in the imagination of their
      hearts.
   He hath put down the mighty from their seats,
   and exalted them of low degree.
   He hath filled the hungry with good things;
   and the rich he hath sent empty away. He hath holpen
      his servant Israel, in remembrance of his mercy; As
      he spake to our fathers, to Abraham, and to his seed
      forever.

THE MAGNIFICAT, LUKE 1:46–55

BLESSED be the Lord God of Israel;
for he hath visited and redeemed his people,
And hath raised up a horn of salvation for us
in the house of his servant David;
as he spake by the mouth of his holy prophets,
which have been since the world began:
that we should be saved from our enemies,
and from the hand of all that hate us;
to perform the mercy promised to our fathers,
and to remember his holy covenant;
the oath which he sware to our father Abraham,
that he would grant unto us,
that we, being delivered out of the hand of our enemies,
might serve him without fear,
in holiness and righteousness before him,
all the days of our life.

And thou, child, shalt be called the prophet of the Highest:
for thou shalt go before the face of the Lord to prepare his
        ways;
to give knowledge of salvation unto his people by the
        remission of their sins,
through the tender mercy of our God;
whereby the dayspring from on high hath visited us,
to give light to them that sit in darkness
and in the shadow of death,
to guide our feet into the way of peace.

THE BENEDICTUS, LUKE 1:68–79

FEAR not: for, behold, I bring you good tidings of great
        joy,
which shall be to all people.

For unto you is born this day in the city of David a Savior,
which is Christ the Lord.
And this shall be a sign unto you;
Ye shall find the babe wrapped in swaddling clothes, lying
in a manger.
And suddenly there was with the angel a multitude of the
heavenly host praising God, and saying,
Glory to God in the highest,
And on earth peace, goodwill toward men.

THE GLORIA OF THE ANGELS, LUKE 2:10–14

LORD, now lettest thou thy servant depart in peace,
according to thy word:
for mine eyes have seen thy salvation, which thou hast
prepared before the face of all people;
a light to lighten the Gentiles, and the glory of thy people
Israel.

THE NUNC DIMITTIS, LUKE 2:29–32

BLESSED be the King that cometh in the name of the
Lord:
peace in heaven, and glory in the highest.

LUKE 19:38

HOSANNA to the Son of David:
Blessed is he that cometh in the name of the Lord;
Hosanna in the highest.

MATTHEW 21:9

HOSANNA;
Blessed is he that cometh in the name of the Lord:
Blessed be the kingdom of our father David,
that cometh in the name of the Lord:
Hosanna in the highest.

MARK 11:9–10

IN the beginning was the Word,
and the Word was with God,
and the Word was God.
The same was in the beginning with God.
All things were made by him;
and without him was not any thing made that was made.
In him was life;
and the life was the light of men.
And the light shineth in darkness;
and the darkness comprehended it not.

There was a man sent from God, whose name was
    John.
The same came for a witness,
to bear witness of the Light,
that all men through him might believe.

He was not that Light, but was sent to bear witness of that
　　　Light.
That was the true Light,
which lighteth every man that cometh into the world.
He was in the world,
and the world was made by him,
and the world knew him not.
He came unto his own,
and his own received him not.
But as many as received him,
to them gave he power to become the sons of God,
even to them that believe on his name:
Which were born, not of blood,
nor of the will of the flesh,
nor of the will of man,
but of God.
And the Word was made flesh,
and dwelt among us,
(and we beheld his glory,
the glory as of the only begotten of the Father,)
full of grace and truth.

　　　John bare witness of him, and cried, saying,
This was he of whom I spake,
he that cometh after me is preferred before me;
for he was before me.
And of his fullness have all we received,
and grace for grace.
For the law was given by Moses,
but grace and truth came by Jesus Christ.
No man hath seen God at any time;
the only begotten Son,
which is in the bosom of the Father,
he hath declared him.

THE HYMN OF JOHN, JOHN 1:1–18

LET this mind be in you, which was also in Christ Jesus:

Who, being in the form of God,
thought it not robbery to be equal with God:
but made himself of no reputation,
and took upon him the form of a servant,
and was made in the likeness of men:
and being found in fashion as a man, he humbled himself,
and became obedient unto death,
even the death of the cross.
Wherefore God also hath highly exalted him,
and given him a name which is above every name:
that at the name of Jesus every knee should bow,
of things in heaven,
and things in earth,
and things under the earth;
and that every tongue should confess
that Jesus Christ is Lord,
to the glory of God the Father.

PHILIPPIANS 2:6–11

THOUGH I speak with the tongues of men and of angels,
and have not charity,
I am become as sounding brass, or a tinkling cymbal.
And though I have the gift of prophecy,
and understand all mysteries, and all knowledge;
and though I have all faith,
so that I could remove mountains,
and have not charity,
I am nothing.
And though I bestow all my goods to feed the poor,
and though I give my body to be burned,
and have not charity,

it profiteth me nothing.
Charity suffereth long, and is kind;
charity envieth not;
charity vaunteth not itself,
is not puffed up.
Doth not behave itself unseemly,
seeketh not her own,
is not easily provoked,
thinketh no evil;
Rejoiceth not in iniquity,
but rejoiceth in the truth;
Beareth all things,
believeth all things,
hopeth all things,
endureth all things.
Charity never faileth:
but whether there be prophecies, they shall fail;
whether there be tongues, they shall cease;
whether there be knowledge, it shall vanish away.
For we know in part,
and we prophesy in part.
But when that which is perfect is come,
then that which is in part shall be done away.
When I was a child,
I spake as a child,
I understood as a child,
I thought as a child:
but when I became a man,
I put away childish things.
For now we see through a glass, darkly;
but then face to face:
now I know in part;
but then shall I know even as also I am known.
And now abideth faith, hope, charity, these three;
but the greatest of these is charity.

1 CORINTHIANS 13:1–13

BUT to us there is but one God, the Father,
of whom are all things, and we in him;
and one Lord Jesus Christ,
by whom are all things, and we by him.

1 CORINTHIANS 8:6

WHO shall separate us from the love of Christ?
Shall tribulation,
or distress,
or persecution,
or famine,
or nakedness,
or peril,
or sword?
    As it is written,
for thy sake we are killed all the day long;
we are accounted as sheep for the slaughter.
Nay, in all these things we are more than conquerors
through him that loved us.

For I am persuaded, that neither death,
nor life,
nor angels,
nor principalities,
nor powers,
nor things present,
nor things to come,
nor height,
nor depth,
nor any other creature,
shall be able to separate us from the love of God,
which is in Christ Jesus our Lord.

ROMANS 8:35–39

AND that, knowing the time,
that now it is high time to awake out of sleep:
for now is our salvation nearer than when we believed.
The night is far spent,
the day is at hand:
let us therefore cast off the works of darkness,
and let us put on the armor of light.

ROMANS 13:11–12

NOW to him that is of power to stablish you according to
    my gospel,
and the preaching of Jesus Christ, according to the
    revelation of the mystery,
which was kept secret since the world began, but now is
    made manifest,
and by the Scriptures of the prophets, according to the
    commandment of the everlasting God,
made known to all nations for the obedience of faith:
to God only wise, be glory through Jesus Christ forever.
Amen.

ROMANS 16:25–27

Who is the image of the invisible God,
the firstborn of every creature:
For by him were all things created,
that are in heaven,
and that are in earth,
visible and invisible,
whether they be thrones,
or dominions,
or principalities,
or powers:
all things were created by him,
and for him:
And he is before all things,
and by him all things consist:
And he is the head of the body, the church:
who is the beginning,
the firstborn from the dead;
that in all things he might have the preeminence.
For it pleased the Father
that in him should all fullness dwell;
and, having made peace through the blood of his cross,
by him to reconcile all things unto himself;
by him, I say, whether they be things in earth,
or things in heaven.

COLOSSIANS 1:15–20

Wherefore he saith,
awake thou that sleepest,
and arise from the dead,
and Christ shall give thee light.

EPHESIANS 5:14

ENDEAVORING to keep the unity of the Spirit
in the bond of peace.
There is one body,
and one Spirit,
even as ye are called
in one hope of your calling;
One Lord,
one faith,
one baptism,
One God and Father of all,
who is above all,
and through all,
and in you all.

EPHESIANS 4:3–6

BUT ye are come unto Mount Zion,
and unto the city of the living God, the heavenly Jerusalem,
and to an innumerable company of angels,
to the general assembly and church of the firstborn, which
        are written in heaven,
and to God the judge of all,
and to the spirits of just men made perfect,
and to Jesus the mediator of the new covenant,
and to the blood of sprinkling,
that speaketh better things than that of Abel.

HEBREWS 12:22–24

IF any man speak, let him speak as the oracles of God;
if any man minister, let him do it as of the ability which
      God giveth;
that God in all things may be glorified through Jesus
      Christ:
to whom be praise and dominion for ever and ever.
Amen.

1 PETER 4:11

BUT the God of all grace,
who hath called us unto his eternal glory by Christ Jesus,
after that ye have suffered a while,
make you perfect, stablish, strengthen, settle you.
To him be glory and dominion for ever and ever.
Amen.

1 PETER 5:10–11

WHO did no sin, neither was guile found in his mouth:
Who, when he was reviled, reviled not again;
when he suffered, he threatened not; but committed himself
      to him that judgeth righteously:
Who his own self bare our sins in his own body on the
      tree, that we, being dead to sins, should live unto
      righteousness:
by whose stripes ye were healed.
For ye were as sheep going astray; but are now returned
      unto the Shepherd and Bishop of your souls.

1 PETER 2:22–25

FOR Christ also hath once suffered for sins,
the just for the unjust,
that he might bring us to God,
being put to death in the flesh,
but quickened by the Spirit:
By which also he went and preached unto the spirits in
      prison;
Which sometime were disobedient,
when once the long-suffering of God waited in the days of
      Noah,
while the Ark was a preparing,
wherein few, that is, eight souls were saved by water.
The like figure whereunto even baptism doth also now save
      us,
(not the putting away of the filth of the flesh,
but the answer of a good conscience toward God,)
by the resurrection of Jesus Christ:
Who is gone into heaven,
and is on the right hand of God;
angels and authorities and powers being made subject unto
      him.

1 PETER 3:18–22

GOD resisteth the proud,
    but giveth grace to the humble.
Submit yourselves therefore to God
    that he may exalt you.
Resist the Devil
    and he will flee from you,
Draw nigh to God
    and he will draw nigh to you.

1 PETER 5:5–9 AND JAMES 4:6–10
(COMPOSITE RECONSTRUCTION)

BLESSED be the God
  and Father of our Lord Jesus Christ!
According to his abundant mercy,
  he hath begotten us
unto a lively hope
  by the resurrection of Jesus Christ from the dead,
to an inheritance incorruptible
  reserved in heaven,
unto salvation ready
  to be revealed in the last time.

1 PETER 1:3–5 AND TITUS 3:4–7
(COMPOSITE RECONSTRUCTION)

NOW unto the King eternal,
immortal,
invisible,
the only wise God,
be honor and glory for ever and ever.
Amen

1 TIMOTHY 1:17

AND without controversy great is the mystery of
    godliness:
God was manifest in the flesh,
justified in the Spirit,
seen of angels,
preached unto the Gentiles,
believed on in the world,
received up into glory.

1 TIMOTHY 3:16

THOU art worthy, O Lord,
to receive glory and honor and power:
for thou hast created all things,
and for thy pleasure they are and were created.

REVELATION 4:11

WORTHY is the Lamb that was slain to receive power,
and riches,
and wisdom,
and strength,
and honor,
and glory,
and blessing.

And every creature which is in heaven,
and on the earth,
and under the earth,
and such as are in the sea,
and all that are in them,
heard I saying, blessing,
and honor,
and glory,
and power,
be unto him that sitteth upon the throne . . .

REVELATION 5:12–13

WE give thee thanks, O Lord God Almighty,
which art, and wast, and art to come;
because thou hast taken to thee thy great power, and hast
      reigned.

And the nations were angry,
and thy wrath is come,
and the time of the dead,
that they should be judged,
and that thou shouldest give reward unto thy servants the
      prophets,
and to the saints,
and them that fear thy name,
small and great;
and shouldest destroy them which destroy the earth.

REVELATION 11:17–18

GREAT and marvelous are thy works, Lord God
      Almighty;
just and true are thy ways, thou King of saints.

Who shall not fear thee, O Lord, and glorify thy name?
For thou only art holy:
for all nations shall come and worship before thee;
for thy judgments are made manifest.

REVELATION 15:3–4

JESUS Christ, who is the faithful witness,
and the first-begotten of the dead,
and the prince of the kings of the earth.

Unto him that loved us,
and washed us from our sins in his own blood,
and hath made us kings and priests unto God and his
      Father;
to him be glory and dominion
for ever and ever. Amen.

Behold, he cometh with clouds;
and every eye shall see him,
and they also which pierced him:
and all kindreds of the earth shall wail because of him.
Even so, amen.

I am alpha and omega,
the beginning and the ending, saith the Lord,
which is, and which was, and which is to come,
the almighty.

REVELATION 1:5–8

I.

THOU art worthy to take the book,
and to open the seals thereof:
for thou wast slain,
and hast redeemed us to God by thy blood
out of every kindred,
and tongue,
and people,
and nation;
and hast made us unto our God kings and priests:
and we shall reign on the earth.

And I beheld,
and I heard the voice of many angels round about the
        throne,
and the beasts,
and the elders:
and the number of them was ten thousand times ten
        thousand,
and thousands of thousands.

II.

Worthy is the Lamb that was slain
to receive power,
and riches,
and wisdom,
and strength,
and honor,
and glory,
and blessing.

III.

Blessing,
and honor,
and glory,
and power,
be unto him that sitteth upon the throne,
and unto the Lamb
for ever and ever.

And the four beasts said, amen.
And the four and twenty elders fell down
and worshiped him that liveth
for ever and ever.

REVELATION 5:9–14

NOW is come salvation,
and strength,
and the kingdom of our God,
and the power of his Christ:
for the accuser of our brethren is cast down,
which accused them before our God day and night.

And they overcame him by the blood of the Lamb,
and by the word of their testimony;
and they loved not their lives unto the death.

Therefore rejoice, ye heavens,
and ye that dwell in them.
Woe to the inhabiters of the earth and of the sea!
For the devil is come down unto you, having great wrath,
because he knoweth that he hath but a short time.

REVELATION 12:10–12

BABYLON the great is fallen, is fallen,
and is become the habitation of devils,
and the hold of every foul spirit,
and a cage of every unclean and hateful bird.
For all nations have drunk of the wine of the wrath of her
       fornication,
and the kings of the earth have committed fornication
       with her,
and the merchants of the earth are waxed rich through the
       abundance of her delicacies. . . .

Come out of her, my people,
that ye be not partakers of her sins,
and that ye receive not of her plagues.
For her sins have reached unto heaven,

and God hath remembered her iniquities.
Reward her even as she rewarded you,
and double unto her double according to her works:
in the cup which she hath filled, fill to her double.
How much she hath glorified herself,
and lived deliciously,
so much torment and sorrow give her:
for she saith in her heart,
I sit a queen,
and am no widow,
and shall see no sorrow.
Therefore shall her plagues come in one day,
death, and mourning, and famine;
and she shall be utterly burned with fire:
for strong is the Lord God who judgeth her.
And the kings of the earth,
who have committed fornication and lived deliciously
        with her,
shall bewail her,
and lament for her,
when they shall see the smoke of her burning,
Standing afar off for the fear of her torment,
saying, Alas, alas, that great city Babylon, that mighty city!
for in one hour is thy judgment come.
And the merchants of the earth shall weep and mourn
        over her;
for no man buyeth their merchandise anymore:
The merchandise of gold,
and silver,
and precious stones,
and of pearls,
and fine linen,
and purple,
and silk,
and scarlet,
and all thyine wood,

and all manner vessels of ivory,
and all manner vessels of most precious wood,
and of brass,
and iron,
and marble,
and cinnamon,
and odors,
and ointments,
and frankincense,
and wine,
and oil,
and fine flour,
and wheat,
and beasts,
and sheep,
and horses,
and chariots,
and slaves,
and souls of men.

And the fruits that thy soul lusted after are departed
from thee,
and all things which were dainty and goodly are departed
from thee,
and thou shalt find them no more at all.
The merchants of these things,
which were made rich by her,
shall stand afar off for the fear of her torment,
weeping and wailing,
and saying, Alas, alas, that great city,
that was clothed in fine linen,
and purple,
and scarlet,
and decked with gold,
and precious stones,
and pearls!

For in one hour so great riches is come to nought.
And every shipmaster,
and all the company in ships,
and sailors,
and as many as trade by sea,
stood afar off,
And cried when they saw the smoke of her burning,
          saying,
What city is like unto this great city!
And they cast dust on their heads,
and cried, weeping and wailing, saying,
Alas, alas, that great city,
wherein were made rich all that had ships in the sea by
          reason of her costliness!
for in one hour is she made desolate.
Rejoice over her, thou heaven,
and ye holy apostles and prophets;
for God hath avenged you on her. . . .

          Thus with violence shall that great city Babylon be
          thrown down,
and shall be found no more at all.
And the voice of harpers,
and musicians,
and of pipers,
and trumpeters,
shall be heard no more at all in thee;
and no craftsman, of whatsoever craft he be,
shall be found anymore in thee;
and the sound of a millstone shall be heard no more at all in
          thee;
and the light of a candle shall shine no more at all in thee;
and the voice of the bridegroom and of the bride shall be
          heard no more at all in thee:
for thy merchants were the great men of the earth;
for by thy sorceries were all nations deceived.

REVELATION 18:2–23

ALLELUIA;
Salvation, and glory, and honor, and power,
unto the Lord our God:
For true and righteous are his judgments;
for he hath judged the great whore,
which did corrupt the earth with her fornication,
and hath avenged the blood of his servants at her
      hand. . . .

    Alleluia.

    Amen; Alleluia.

    Praise our God,
all ye his servants,
and ye that fear him,
both small and great.

    Alleluia:
for the Lord God omnipotent reigneth.

    Let us be glad and rejoice,
and give honor to him:
for the marriage of the Lamb is come,
and his wife hath made herself ready.
And to her was granted that she should be arrayed in fine
      linen, clean and white:
for the fine linen is the righteousness of saints.
Blessed are they which are called unto the marriage supper
      of the Lamb.

REVELATION 19:1–9

I am the root and the offspring of David,
and the bright and morning star.
And the Spirit and the bride say, Come.
And let him that heareth say, Come.
And let him that is athirst come.
And whosoever will, let him take the water of life
      freely. . . .

Surely I come quickly: Amen.
Even so, come, Lord Jesus.

REVELATION 22:16–17, 20

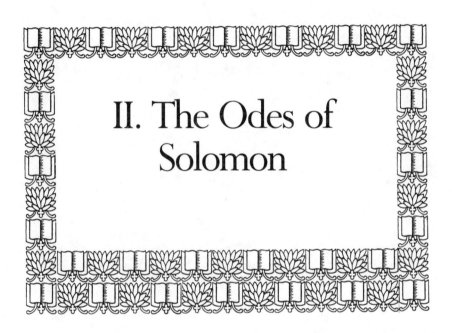

II. The Odes of Solomon

I poured out praise to the Lord,
Because I am His own.

And I will recite His holy ode,
Because my heart is with Him.

ODE 26

THE Odes of Solomon comprise the first extant Christian hymn book. The attribution to Solomon is almost certainly inspired by the Song of Solomon in the scriptures, where Solomon's reputation as a poet is established. In addition, in their naturalistic imagery ("Because my breasts and my pleasure are with thee"—Ode 14) and frequent reference to "the beloved," these odes are reminiscent of the type of love poems we find in the Song of Solomon. Yet the main literary genre according to which they are patterned is clearly the Old Testament Psalms.

Though they cannot be dated exactly, this beautiful collection of hymns was very likely gathered during the late first or very early second century. Their formal dependence upon the psalms underscores the primary relationship between early Christian worship and Jewish liturgical conventions. Other parallels, especially in theological imagery (light versus darkness; the Way; living waters), can be made between these odes and certain of the Dead Sea Scrolls, a body of literature that reflects another tradition of sectarian Judaism, one running parallel to the emergence of Jewish Christianity (for example in odes 30, 39). Though the New Testament is not a direct source (which also suggests a very early date for these hymns), many scholars see parallels between the Odes of Solomon and the Johannine tradition (for example, "For the dwelling place of the Word is man / and his truth is love"—Ode 12), some even suggesting that the Odes and the Gospel of John were written at very close to the same time and initially shared within the same Christian community, most probably Antioch.

As you read these odes, note the way in which traditional Jewish forms have been adapted explicitly to serve as vehicles for the transmission and affirmation of early Christian theological claims, especially the relationship of salvation history to the person of Christ (for example in odes 7, 12, 39).

Also, we find here for the first time hints of a tradition that will later be developed both in Gnostic Christian hymnody (see chapters 4 and 5) and in Syriac orthodox traditions as well (see chapter 6), namely that to enter the circle of salvation, even to participate in the Godhead, the most effective and fitting entryway is song (for example, "I will open my mouth, / and his spirit will speak through me"—Ode 16). Thus hymn singing becomes the most appropriate and important vocation of the worshiper.

THE Lord is on my head like a crown,
And I shall never be without him.

Plaited for me is the crown of truth,
And it caused thy branches to blossom in me.

For it is not like a parched crown that blossoms not;

But thou livest upon my head,
And have blossomed upon me.

Thy fruits are full and complete;
They are full of thy salvation.

ODE 1

I am putting on the love of the Lord.

And his members are with him,
And I am dependent on them; and he loves me.

For I should not have known how to love the Lord,
If he had not continuously loved me.

Who is able to distinguish love,
Except him who is loved?

I love the Beloved and I myself love him,
And where his rest is, there also am I.

And I shall be no stranger,
Because there is no jealousy with the Lord Most High and
      Merciful.

I have been united to him, because the lover has found the
      Beloved,
Because I love him that is the Son, I shall become a son.

Indeed he who is joined to him who is immortal,
Truly shall be immortal.

And he who delights in the Life
Will become living.

This is the Spirit of the Lord, which is not false,
Which teaches the sons of men to know his ways.

Be wise and understanding and vigilant.

   Hallelujah.

ODE 3

As the wind glides through the harp
And the strings speak,

So the Spirit of the Lord speaks through my members,
And I speak through his love.

For he destroys whatever is alien,
And everything is of the Lord.

For thus it was from the beginning,
And will be until the end.

So that nothing shall be contrary,
And nothing shall rise up against him.

The Lord has multiplied his knowledge,
And he was zealous that those things should be known
      which through his grace have been given to us.

And his praise he gave us on account of his name,
Our spirits praise his Holy Spirit.

For there went forth a stream, and it became a river great
      and broad;
Indeed it carried away everything, and it shattered and
      brought it to the Temple.

And the restraints of men were not able to restrain it,
Nor even the arts of them who habitually restrain water.

For it spread over the surface of all the earth,
And it filled everything.

Then all the thirsty upon the earth drank,
And thirst was relieved and quenched;

For from the Most High the drink was given.

Blessed, therefore, are the ministers of that drink,
Who have been entrusted with his water.

They have refreshed the parched lips,
And have aroused the paralyzed will.

Even living persons who were about to expire,
They have held back from death.

And limbs which had collapsed,
They have restored and set up.

They gave strength for their coming,
And light for their eyes.

Because everyone recognized them as the Lord's,
And lived by the living water of eternity.

Hallelujah.

ODE 6

As is the course of anger over wickedness,
So is the course of joy over the Beloved;
And brings in of its fruits unhindered.

My joy is the Lord and my course is toward him,
This path of mine is beautiful.

For there is a helper for me, the Lord.
He has generously shown himself to me in his simplicity,
Because his kindness has diminished his dreadfulness.

He became like me, that I might receive him.
In form he was considered like me, that I might put him
      on.

And I trembled not when I saw him,
Because he was gracious to me.

Like my nature he became, that I might understand him.
And like my form, that I might not turn away from him.

The Father of knowledge
Is the Word of knowledge.

He who created wisdom
Is wiser than his works.

And he who created me when yet I was not
Knew what I would do when I came into being.

On account of this he was gracious to me in his abundant
      grace,
And allowed me to ask from him and to benefit from his
      sacrifice.

For he it is who is incorrupt,
The perfection of the worlds and their Father.

He has allowed him to appear to them that are his own;
In order that they may recognize him that made them,
And not suppose that they came of themselves.

For toward knowledge he has set his way,
He has widened it and lengthened it and brought it to
      complete perfection.

And has set over it the traces of his light,
And it proceeded from the beginning until the end.

For by him he was served,
And he was pleased by the Son.

And because of his salvation he will possess everything.
And the Most High will be known by his holy ones:

To announce to those who have songs of the coming of the
      Lord,
That they may go forth to meet him and may sing to him,
With joy and with the harp of many tones.

The seers shall go before Him,
And they shall be seen before Him.

And they shall praise the Lord in his love,
Because he is near and does see.

And hatred shall be removed from the earth,
And with jealousy it shall be drowned.

For ignorance was destroyed upon it,
Because the knowledge of the Lord arrived upon it.

Let the singers sing the grace of the Lord Most High,
And let them bring their songs.

And let their heart be like the day,
And their gentle voices like the majestic beauty of the Lord.

And let there not be anyone who breathes
That is without knowledge or voice.

For he gave a mouth to his creation:
To open the voice of the mouth toward him,
And to praise him.

Confess his power
And declare his grace.

   Hallelujah.

ODE 7

OPEN, open your hearts to the exultation of the Lord,
And let your love abound from the heart to the lips.

In order to bring forth fruits to the Lord, a holy life;
And to talk with watchfulness in his light.

Rise up and stand erect,
You who sometimes were brought low.

You who were in silence, speak,
For your mouth has been opened.

You who were despised, from henceforth be lifted up,
For your righteousness has been lifted up;

For the right hand of the Lord is with you,
And he will be your Helper.

And peace was prepared for you,
Before what may be your war.

(Christ Speaks)

Hear the word of truth,
And receive the knowledge of the Most High.

Your flesh may not understand that which I am about to
    say to you;
Nor your garment that which I am about to show you.

Keep my mystery, you who are kept by it;
Keep my faith, you who are kept by it.

And understand my knowledge, you who know me in
    truth;
Love me with affection, you who love;

For I turn not my face from my own,
Because I know them.

And before they had existed,
I recognized them;
And imprinted a seal on their faces.

I fashioned their members,
And my own breasts I prepared for them,
That they might drink my holy milk and live by it.

I am pleased by them,
And am not ashamed by them.

For my workmanship are they,
And the strength of my thoughts.

Therefore who can stand against my work?
Or who is not subject to them?

I willed and fashioned mind and heart,
And they are my own.
And upon my right hand I have set my elect ones.

And my righteousness goes before them,
And they shall not be deprived of my name;
For it is with them.

(The Odist Himself Speaks)

Pray and increase,
And abide in the love of the Lord;

And you who are loved in the Beloved,
And you who are kept in him who lives,
And you who are saved in him who was saved.

And you shall be found incorrupt in all ages,
On account of the name of your Father.

Hallelujah.

ODE 8

MY heart was pruned and its flower appeared,
Then grace sprang up in it,
And it produced fruits for the Lord.

For the Most High circumcised me by his Holy Spirit,
Then he uncovered my inward being toward him,
And filled me with his love.

And his circumcising became my salvation,
And I ran in the way, in his peace,
In the way of truth.

From the beginning until the end
I received his knowledge.

And I was established upon the rock of truth,
Where he had set me.

And speaking waters touched my lips
From the fountain of the Lord generously.

And so I drank and became intoxicated,
From the living water that does not die.

And my intoxication did not cause ignorance;
But I abandoned vanity,

And turned toward the Most High, my God,
And was enriched by his favors.

And I rejected the folly cast upon the earth,
And stripped it off and cast it from me.

And the Lord renewed me with his garment,
And possessed me by his light.

And from above he gave me immortal rest,
And I became like the land that blossoms and rejoices in its
       fruits.

And the Lord is like the sun
Upon the face of the land.

My eyes were enlightened,
And my face received the dew;

And my breath was refreshed
By the pleasant fragrance of the Lord.

And He took me to his Paradise,
Wherein is the wealth of the Lord's pleasure.

I beheld blooming and fruit-bearing trees,
And self-grown was their crown.

Their branches were sprouting
And their fruits were shining.

From an immortal land were their roots.

And a river of gladness was irrigating them,

And round about them in the land of eternal life.

Then I worshiped the Lord because of his magnificence.

And I said, Blessed, O Lord, are they
Who are planted in thy land,
And who have a place in thy Paradise;

And who grow in the growth of thy trees,
And have passed from darkness into light.

Behold, all thy laborers are fair,
They who work good works,
And turn from wickedness to thy pleasantness.

For they turned away from themselves the bitterness of the
        trees,
When they were planted in thy land.

And everyone was like thy remnant.
Blessed are the workers of thy waters,
Because it is an eternal memorial for thy faithful servants.

Indeed, there is much room in thy Paradise.
And there is nothing in it which is barren,
But everything is filled with fruit.

Glory be to thee, O God, the delight of Paradise forever.

   Hallelujah.

ODE 11

HE has filled me with words of truth,
That I may proclaim him.

And like the flowing of waters, truth flows from my
      mouth,
And my lips declare his fruits.

And he has caused his knowledge to abound in me,
Because the mouth of the Lord is the true Word,
And the entrance of his light.

And the Most High has given him to his generations,
Which are the interpreters of his beauty,
   And the narrators of his glory,
   And the confessors of his purpose,
   And the preachers of his mind,
   And the teachers of his works.

For the subtlety of the Word is inexpressible,
And like his utterance so also is his swiftness and his
      acuteness,
For limitless is his progression.

He never falls but remains standing,
And one cannot comprehend his descent or his way.

For as his work is, so is his expectation,
For he is the light and dawning of thought.

And by him the generations spoke to one another,
And those that were silent acquired speech.

And from him came love and equality,
And they spoke one to another that which was theirs.

And they were stimulated by the Word,
And knew him who made them,
Because they were in harmony.

For the mouth of the Most High spoke to them,
And his exposition prospered through him.

For the dwelling place of the Word is man,
And his truth is love.

Blessed are they who by means of him have perceived
      everything,
And have known the Lord in his truth.

  Hallelujah.

ODE 12

BEHOLD, the Lord is our mirror.
Open your eyes and see them in him.

And learn the manner of your face,
Then declare praises to his Spirit.

And wipe the paint from your face,
And love his holiness and put it on.

Then you will be unblemished at all times with him.

  Hallelujah.

ODE 13

As the eyes of a son upon his father,
So are my eyes, O Lord, at all times toward thee.

Because my breasts and my pleasure are with thee.

Turn not aside thy mercies from me, O Lord;
And take not thy kindness from me.

Stretch out to me, my Lord, at all times, thy right hand,
And be to me a guide till the end according to thy will.

Let me be pleasing before thee, because of thy glory,
And because of thy name let me be saved from the Evil
          One.

And let thy gentleness, O Lord, abide with me,
And the fruits of thy love.

Teach me the odes of thy truth,
That I may produce fruits in thee.

And open to me the harp of thy Holy Spirit,
So that with every note I may praise thee, O Lord.

And according to the multitude of thy mercies, so grant
          unto me,
And hasten to grant our petitions.
For thou art sufficient for all our needs.

   Hallelujah.

ODE 14

As the occupation of the ploughman is the ploughshare,
And the occupation of the helmsman is the steering of the
    ship,
So also my occupation is the psalm of the Lord by his
    hymns.

My art and my service are in his hymns,
Because his love has nourished my heart,
And his fruits he poured unto my lips.

For my love is the Lord;
Hence I will sing unto him.

For I am strengthened by his praises,
And I have faith in him.

I will open my mouth,
And his spirit will speak through me
The glory of the Lord and his beauty,

The work of his hands,
And the labor of his fingers;

For the multitude of his mercies,
And the strength of his Word.

For the Word of the Lord investigates that which is
    invisible,
And reveals his thought.

For the eye sees his works,
And the ear hears his thought.

It is he who made the earth broad,
And placed the waters in the sea.

He expanded the heaven,
And fixed the stars.

And he fixed the creation and set it up,
Then he rested from his works.

And created things run according to their courses,
And work their works,
For they can neither cease nor fail.

And the hosts are subject to his Word.

The reservoir of light is the sun,
And the reservoir of darkness is the night.

For he made the sun for the day so that it will be light;
But night brings darkness over the face of the earth.

And by their portion one from another
They complete the beauty of God.

And there is nothing outside of the Lord,
Because he was before anything came to be.

And the worlds are by his Word,
And by the thought of his heart.

Praise and honor to his name.

    Hallelujah.

ODE 16

JOY is for the holy ones.
And who shall put it on but they alone?

Grace is for the elect ones.
And who shall receive it but they who trusted in it from
    the beginning?

Love is for the elect ones.
And who shall put it on but they who possessed it from the
    beginning?

Walk in the knowledge of the Lord,
And you will know the grace of the Lord generously;
Both for his exultation and for the perfection of his
    knowledge.

And his thought was like a letter,
And his will descended from on high.

And it was sent like an arrow
Which from a bow has been forcibly shot.

And many hands rushed to the letter,
In order to catch it, then take and read it,

But it escaped from their fingers;
And they were afraid of it and of the seal which was
        upon it.

Because they were not allowed to loosen its seal;
For the power which was over the seal was greater than
        they.

But those who saw the letter went after it;
That they might learn where it would land,
And who should read it,
And who should hear it.

But a wheel received it,
And it came over it.

And a sign was with it,
Of the kingdom and of providence.

And everything which was disturbing the wheel,
It mowed and cut down.

And it restrained a multitude of adversaries;
And bridged rivers.

And it crossed over and uprooted many forests,
And made an open way.

The head went down to the feet,
Because unto the feet ran the wheel,
And whatever had come upon it.

The letter was one of command,
And hence all regions were gathered together.

And there was seen at its head, the head which was
        revealed,
Even the Son of Truth from the Most High Father.

And he inherited and possessed everything,
And then the scheming of the many ceased.

Then all the seducers became headstrong and fled,
And the persecutors became extinct and were blotted out.

And the letter became a large volume,
Which was entirely written by the finger of God.

And the name of the Father was upon it;
And of the Son and of the Holy Spirit,
To rule for ever and ever.

Hallelujah.

ODE 23

I poured out praise to the Lord,
Because I am his own.

And I will recite his holy ode,
Because my heart is with him.

For his harp is in my hand,
And the odes of his rest shall not be silent.

I will call unto him with all my heart,
I will praise and exalt him with all my members.

For from the east and unto the west
Is his praise;

Also from the south and unto the north
Is his thanksgiving.

Even from the crest of the summits and unto their
        extremity
Is his perfection.

Who can write the odes of the Lord,
Or who can read them?

Or who can train himself for life,
So that he himself may be saved?

Or who can press upon the Most High,
So that he would recite from his mouth?

Who can interpret the wonders of the Lord?
Though he who interprets will be destroyed,
Yet that which was interpreted will remain.

For it suffices to perceive and be satisfied,
For the odists stand in serenity;

Like a river which has an increasingly gushing spring,
And flows to the relief of them that seek it.

Hallelujah.

ODE 26

FILL for yourselves water from the living fountain of the
        Lord,
Because it has been opened for you.

And come all you thirsty and take a drink,
And rest beside the fountain of the Lord.

Because it is pleasing and sparkling,
And perpetually refreshes the self.

For much sweeter is its water than honey,
And the honeycomb of bees is not to be compared with it;

Because it flowed from the lips of the Lord,
And it named from the heart of the Lord.

And it came boundless and invisible,
And until it was set in the middle they knew it not.

Blessed are they who have drunk from it,
And have refreshed themselves by it.

   Hallelujah.

ODE 30

THERE is no hard way where there is a simple heart;
Nor barrier for upright thoughts,

Nor whirlwind in the depth of the enlightened thought.

Where one is surrounded on every side by pleasing country,
There is nothing divided in him.

The likeness of that which is below
Is that which is above.

For everything is from above,
And from below there is nothing,
But it is believed to be by those in whom there is no
        understanding.

Grace has been revealed for your salvation.
Believe and live and be saved.

   Hallelujah.

ODE 34

RAGING rivers are like the power of the Lord;
They send headlong those who despise him.

And entangle their paths,
And destroy their crossings.

And snatch their bodies,
And corrupt their natures.

For they are more swift than lightnings,
Even more rapid.

But those who cross them in faith
Shall not be disturbed.

And those who walk on them faultlessly
Shall not be shaken.

Because the sign on them is the Lord,
And the sign is the Way for those who cross in the name of
        the Lord.

Therefore, put on the name of the Most High and
        know him,
And you shall cross without danger;
Because rivers shall be obedient to you.

The Lord has bridged them by his Word,
And he walked and crossed them on foot.

And his footsteps stand firm upon the waters, and were not
        destroyed;
But they are like a beam of wood that is constructed on
        truth.

On this side and on that the waves were lifted up,
But the footsteps of our Lord Messiah stand firm.

And they are neither blotted out,
Nor destroyed.

And the Way has been appointed for those who cross over
        after him,
And for those who adhere to the path of his faith;
And who adore his name.

   Hallelujah.

ODE 39

As honey drips from the honeycomb of bees,
And milk flows from the woman who loves her children,
So also is my hope upon thee, O my God.

As a fountain gushes forth its water,
So my heart gushes forth the praise of the Lord,
And my lips bring forth praise to him.

And my tongue becomes sweet by his anthems,
And my members are anointed by his odes.

My face rejoices in his exultation,
And my spirit exults in his love,
And my nature shines in him.

And he who is afraid shall trust in him,
And redemption shall be assured in him.

And his possessions are immortal life,
And those who receive it are incorruptible.

   Hallelujah.

ODE 40

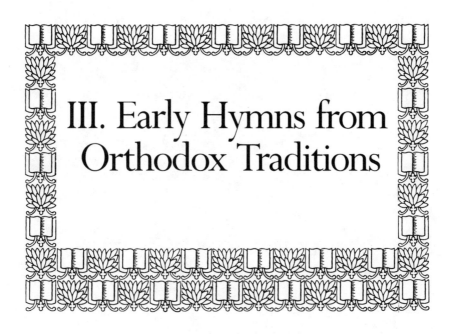

III. Early Hymns from
Orthodox Traditions

A chant celebrates the fear of the Law,
The grace of the Prophets is made known,
The faith of the Gospels is implanted,
The tradition of the Apostles is
        secured, . . .
The grace of the Church waxes jubilant.

THE EPISTLE TO DIOGNETUS

B Y the beginning of the second century, the intimate relationship between hymnody (including liturgical chants and psalmody) and the specifics of Christian theology and practice was already well established. In the writings of the apostolic fathers, the Epistle to Diognetus testifies explicitly to this; in the first extant liturgy, the Didache (included in *The Macmillan Book of Earliest Christian Prayers*), the eucharistic prayer is a catena of hymns; and in the Epistles of Ignatius, there are two Christological hymns reminiscent of those included in the New Testament epistles, but also showing a development toward decidedly credal hymnody.

The hymns in this chapter date from the early second to the early fourth century. Of all the hymns collected in this book, the only one for which the music has survived is the hymn fragment from the Oxyrhynchus Papyrus. In other of the hymns, including the papyri, you will notice the beginning of a trend toward the employment of hymns as a medium for liturgical regimen and doctrinal regimentation: morning and evening hymns; hymns for particular liturgical seasons (Epiphany, Christmas, Easter, and so on); eucharistic and baptismal hymns. Though hinted at in the New Testament hymns, here the importance of hymnody to theological instruction and spiritual discipline is fully manifest. In early Christianity, popular piety was far more dependent upon the repeated incantation of chant and song than upon the study of the scriptures.

The two Easter hymns attributed to Hippolytus suggest further development of the hymn form as a medium for religious instruction, especially in the recounting of salvation history, but the most striking example is the late-second-century Homily on the Pasch, by Melito of Sardis. The utilization of rhythmic language, parallel structure, and repetition, together served to enhance retention of the elements of faith expounded here. Beyond this, it is a stunning piece of literature, an early Christian masterpiece.

Clement of Alexandria's hymns, written at the turn of the third century, demonstrate the influence of classical poetic forms, which will increasingly supplement and in many instances supplant the Jewish precedents for Christian hymnody. Pagan Roman worship practices also began to shape parts of the Christian liturgy. We include the liturgy for the enthonement of Ausonius, a Christian, as counsel of Rome in the mid-fourth century, as an example of hymnody familiar within the Imperial cultus; compare this with the responsive chant of Methodius of Olympus, written perhaps half a century earlier.

We close this chapter with a different type of responsive litany, again not sung but chanted, yet familiar in form to Christians at worship from the third century down to this very day.

I.

THERE is only one physician,
Of flesh, yet spiritual,
Born yet unbegotten,
God incarnate,
Genuine life in the midst of death,
Sprung from Mary as well as God,
First subject to suffering, then beyond it,
Jesus Christ, our Lord.

II.

BE on the alert for Him who is above time,
The Timeless, the Unseen,
The One who became visible for our sakes,
Who was beyond touch and passion,
Yet who for our sakes became subject to suffering,
And endured everything for us.

IGNATIUS OF ANTIOCH

GLORY be to God in the highest,
and upon earth peace,
goodwill among men.
We praise thee,
we sing hymns to thee,
we bless thee,
we glorify thee,
we worship thee by thy great High Priest;
thee who art the true God,
who art the One Unbegotten,
the only inaccessible Being.
For thy great glory,
O Lord and heavenly King,
O God the Father Almighty, O Lord God,
the Father of Christ the immaculate Lamb,
who taketh away the sin of the world,
receive our prayer,
thou that sittest upon the cherubim.
For thou only art holy,
thou only art the Lord Jesus,
the Christ of the God of all created nature,
and our King,
by whom glory,
honor,
and worship be to thee.

GLORIA IN EXCELSIS, APOSTOLIC CONSTITUTIONS

MAY none of God's wonderful works
keep silence, night or morning.
Bright stars, high mountains, the depths of the seas,
sources of rushing rivers:
may all these break into song as we sing

to Father, Son and Holy Spirit.
May all the angels in the heavens reply:
Amen! Amen! Amen!
Power, praise, honor, eternal glory
to God, the only giver of grace.
Amen! Amen! Amen!

OXYRHYNCHUS PAPYRUS

HOLY you are, Lord God Almighty,
Father of our Lord Jesus Christ,
delightful Garden,
kingly Sceptre,
lavish Love,
Hope assured and firm,
Counsel . . .
Holy you are, Lord God,
King of kings and Lord of lords.
You alone have immortality;
you live in light that none can approach,
and no man has ever seen it;
you sit above the cherubim and thrones,
you ride on the wings of the winds;
you created the heavens, the land, the sea
and all that is in them . . .
you make the winds your messengers
and the fiery flames your servants;
you made man like yourself,
an image of yourself you made him;
you measured heaven with the span of your fingers
and the whole earth with the palm of your hand . . .
Fair indeed your works are to you.

BERLIN PAPYRUS

YOU guard the lamb, having taken it upon your shoulder
    and having united it with your flock.
I then recognized that the Son is the shepherd,
I then received the pasture from the Father.
I will travel through the frightful powers without suffering
    anything from them.
Trusting in you, Christ, Blessed One,
I will escape from those who conspire against me.
I will arouse the harpists for you, and perform the holy
    dances.
O, Word of the boundless Father,
To you be glory and power forever.

BERLIN PAPYRUS

AT Bethlehem born,
at Nazareth brought up,
he lived in Galilee.
A sign in the sky; we saw it ourselves.

How the star shone! The shepherds that night
in the fields fell to their knees in amazement and said:
Glory to the Father, Alleluia.
Glory to the Son and Holy Spirit.
Alleluia, Alleluia, Alleluia.

FOYYUM PAPYRUS

THIS is his blood who took flesh
of the Holy Virgin:
Jesus Christ.

This is his blood who was born
of the God-bearing saint:
Jesus Christ.

This is God's blood whom men saw
and demons fled from:
Jesus Christ.

This is his blood who was baptized
in the Jordan by John the forerunner:
Jesus Christ. Amen.

This is his blood who offered himself
a sacrifice for our sins:
Jesus Christ. Amen.

VIENNA PAPYRUS

THIS is the Paschal feast, the Lord's passing:
so cries the Spirit.

No type or telling, this,
no shadow;
Pasch of the Lord it is, and truly.
The blood that is shed is a sign of the blood to be shed,
the first indication of what the Spirit will be,
a glimpse of the great anointing.
"I, seeing the blood, will protect you."

You have indeed protected us, Jesus,
from endless disaster.
You spread your hands like a Father
and fatherlike gave cover with your wings.

Your blood, a God's blood, you poured over the earth,
sealing a blood-bargain
for men because you loved them.
What anger threatened you turned away from us;
instead you gave us back God's friendship.

The heavens may have your spirit, paradise your soul,
but O may the earth have your blood.

This feast of the Spirit
leads the mystic dance through the year.
The Pasch came from God, came from heaven to earth;
from earth it has gone back to heaven.
New is this feast and all-embracing;
all creation assembles at it.

Joy to all creatures, honor, feasting, delight.
Dark death is destroyed
and life is restored everywhere.
The gates of heaven are open.
God has shown himself man,
man has gone up to him a God.
The gates of hell God has shattered,
the bars of Adam's prison broken.
The people of the world below have risen from the dead,
bringing good news:
what was promised is fulfilled.
From the earth has come singing and dancing.

This is God's passing.
Heaven's God, showing no meanness,
has joined us to himself in the Spirit.
The great marriage hall is full of guests,
all dressed for the wedding, no guest rejected
for want of a wedding dress.
The Paschal light is the bright new lamplight,

light that shines from the virgins' lamps.
The light in the soul will never go out.
The fire of grace burns in us all,
spirit, divine,
in our bodies and in our souls,
fed with the oil of Christ.

We pray you, God, our Sovereign, Christ,
King forever in the world of spirits,
stretch out your strong hands over your holy Church
and over the people that will always be yours.
Defend, protect, preserve them,
fight and do battle for them,
subject their enemies to them,
subdue the invisible powers that oppose them,
as you have already subdued those that hate us.
Raise now the sign of victory over us
and grant
that we may sing with Moses the song of triumph.
For yours are victory and power
for ever and ever. Amen.

EASTER HYMN, ATTRIBUTED TO HIPPOLYTUS

Do you honor God? Do you love him?
—here's the very feast for your pleasure.
Are you his servant, knowing his wishes?
—be glad with your Master, share his rejoicing.
Are you worn down with the labor of fasting?
—now is the time of your payment.

Have you been working since early morning?
—now you will be paid what is fair.

Have you been here since the third hour?
—you can be thankful, you will be pleased.

If you came at the sixth hour,
you may approach without fearing:
you will suffer no loss.
Did you linger till the ninth hour?
—come forward without hesitation.
What though you came at the eleventh hour?
—have no fear; it was not too late.

God is a generous Sovereign,
treating the last to come as he treats the first arrival.
He allows all his workmen to rest—
those who began at the eleventh hour,
those who have worked from the first,
He is kind to the latecomer
and sees to the needs of the early,
gives to the one and gives to the other:
honors the deed and praises the motive.

Join, then, all of you, join in our Master's rejoicing.
You who were the first to come, you who came after,
come and collect now your wages.
Rich men and poor men, sing and dance together.
You that are hard on yourselves, you that are easy,
honor this day.
You that have fasted and you that have not,
make merry today.

The meal is ready: come and enjoy it.
The calf is a fat one: you will not go hungry away.
There's kindness for all to partake of and kindness to spare,

Away with pleading of poverty:
the kingdom belongs to us all.

Away with bewailing of failings:
forgiveness has come from the grave.
Away with your fears of dying:
the death of our Savior has freed us from fear.
Death played the master: he has mastered death . . .
The world below had scarcely known him in the flesh
when he rose and left it plunged in bitter mourning.

Isaias knew it would be so.
The world of shadows mourned, he cried, when it
        met you,
mourned at its bringing low, wept at its deluding.
The shadows seized a body and found it was God;
they reached for earth and what they held was heaven;
they took what they could see: it was what no one sees.
Where is death's goad? Where is the shadows' victory?

Christ is risen: the world below is in ruins.
Christ is risen: the spirits of evil are fallen.
Christ is risen: the angels of God are rejoicing.
Christ is risen: the tombs are void of their dead.
Christ has indeed arisen from the dead,
the first of the sleepers.

Glory and power are his for ever and ever. Amen.

EASTER HYMN, ATTRIBUTED TO HIPPOLYTUS

Homily on the Pasch

I.

WE have just read from the Scriptures the story of the
Exodus of the Hebrews. Then we explained the words of
the mystery: how the lamb was sacrificed, how the people
were saved. Understand, then, beloved:

> The mystery of the Pasch
> is new and old,
> eternal and temporal,
> corruptible and incorruptible,
> mortal and immortal.

> Old according to the Law,
> new according to the Word;
> temporal according to the world,
> eternal by grace;
> corruptible by the immolation of the lamb,
> incorruptible by the life of the Lord;
> mortal by his burial in the earth,
> immortal by his resurrection from the dead.

> The Law is old,
> but the Word is new.
> The figure is temporal,
> but grace is eternal.
> The lamb is corruptible,
> but the Lord is incorruptible,
> who had no bone broken as a lamb
> but who rose from the dead as God. . . .

> For the figure has passed away,
> the reality has been revealed:
> in the lamb's place God has come,
> in the sheep's place, the man.

In the man is the Christ
  who contains all things.

For the sacrifice of the Lamb
and the celebration of the Pasch
and the letter of the Law
have been fulfilled in Christ.
Through him was made
everything in the old Law
  and, still more, everything in the new Law.

For the Law has become the Word,
the old has become new
—it goes forth from Zion and from Jerusalem—
and the commandment has become grace,
and the figure has become the reality,
and the lamb has become the Son,
and the sheep has become a man,
  and the man has become God.

Born as Son,
led like a lamb,
sacrificed like a sheep,
buried as a man,
he rises from the dead as God,
being by nature both God and man.

He is all things:
when he judges, he is Law,
when he teaches, Word,
when he saves, grace,
when he begets, father,
when he is begotten, son,
when he suffers, lamb,
when he is buried, man,
when he rises, God.

Such is Jesus Christ!
To him be glory forever! Amen.

II.

Pharaoh wore Egypt like a mourning garment.
Such was the robe woven for the tyrant's body,
such the garment the angel of justice threw about the
    hard-hearted Pharaoh:
mourning that pierces, darkness that thickens, and no
    more children. . . .
Swift and insatiable the death of the firstborn! . . .

If you listen to the story of this astounding tragedy,
amazement will seize you. For here is what enveloped the
Egyptians:

    a vast night
    and a thick darkness,
    and groping death,
    and the exterminating angel,
    and the lower world that swallows up their firstborn.

But listen to something even more astounding and
terrifying: in the darkness that was almost palpable,
insatiable death was hiding. The anguished Egyptians were
groping in the darkness, and groping death was seizing the
firstborn of the Egyptians at the angel's command!
    If anyone, then, was groping about in the darkness, the
angel snatched him away. If a firstborn touched a hidden
body, terror filled his soul and he uttered a frightful wail:

    "Whom is my hand grasping?
    Whom does my soul fear?
    What darkness surrounds my body?

If it be my father, help me!
If it be my mother, comfort me!
If it be my brother, speak to me?
If it be a friend, support me!
If it be an enemy, depart,
for I am a firstborn!"

But before the firstborn falls silent, unending silence
has enveloped him. It whispers to him: "Firstborn, you
belong to me; I, the silence of death, am fated to be
yours! . . ."

One blow and he is dead
who was the fruit,
the firstborn of the Egyptians,
the first one sown,
the first one brought to birth,
desired and coddled:
he has been smashed to the ground.

III.

O unutterable mystery!
The sacrifice of the lamb was the salvation of the
    people,
the death of the lamb brought life to the people,
its blood intimidated the angel!

Tell me, angel, what intimidated you:
the sacrifice of the lamb or the life of the Lord,
the death of the lamb or the prefiguration of the Lord,
the blood of the lamb or the Spirit of the Lord?

Show me what intimidated you.
You saw the mystery of the Lord

in the lot of the lamb,
and the life of the Lord
in the sacrifice of the lamb,
and the figure of the Lord
in the death of the lamb.
That is why you did not strike Israel
but deprived only Egypt of her children.

IV.

The Gospel is the explanation and fulfillment of the
Law, and the Church is the place where the Law comes
true.

The figure was precious before the reality came,
and the parable marvelous before it was explained.
That is, the people were precious
before the Church was established,
and the Law was marvelous
before the light of the Gospel shone.

But when the Church was built
and the Gospel was revealed,
then the figure was emptied out,
for it passed its power on to the reality,
and the Law was fulfilled,
for it passed its power on to the Gospel. . . .

For precious of old was the sacrifice of the Law,
but now it has lost its value
because of the Lord's life.

Precious was the death of the lamb,
but now it has lost its value
because of the salvation of the Lord.

Precious was the blood of the lamb,
but now it has lost its value
because of the Spirit of the Lord.

Precious was the lamb that remained silent,
but now it has lost its value
because of the sinless Son.

Precious was the earthly temple,
but now it has lost its value
because of Christ who is above.

Precious was the earthly Jerusalem,
but now it has lost its value,
because of the Jerusalem that is above.

Precious was the inheritance strictly reserved,
but now it has lost its value
because of the grace generously poured out.

For no longer is there a single place nor the tiniest enclosure where the glory of God has not been established, but his grace has been poured out to the very ends of the earth, and there the almighty God has built his tabernacle, through Jesus Christ.
To him be glory forever! Amen.

V.

The Lord had foreordained an image of his suffering in the persons of the patriarchs and the prophets and the entire people. . . .

If you wish to see the mystery of the Lord,
consider Abel, who was likewise killed,

Isaac, who was likewise fettered,
Joseph, who was likewise sold,
David, who was likewise persecuted,
the prophets, who likewise suffered
    because of Christ.

Consider, finally, the lamb
that was sacrificed in the land of Egypt
and saved Israel by its blood. . . .

Many other predictions were made by the prophets in regard to the mystery of the Pasch, that is, in regard to Jesus Christ.
To him be glory forever! Amen.

VI.

Through his body which was subject to suffering
he put an end to the sufferings of the flesh,
and through his Spirit who cannot die
he slew the death that slays men.

Like a sheep he was led away,
like a lamb he was sacrificed,
he who delivered us
from slavery to the world,
as from another Egypt,
and who liberated us
from slavery to the devil,
as from the hand of Pharaoh,
and who impressed upon our souls
the seal of his own blood.

It is he who covered death with shame
and threw the Devil into mourning
as Moses did Pharaoh.

It is he who struck down iniquity
and deprived injustice of its children
as Moses did Egypt.

It is he who led us out
from slavery to freedom,
from darkness to light,
from death to life,
from tyranny to eternal kingship.

He is the Pasch of our salvation.
It is he who endured many sufferings
It is he who was slain in Abel;
in Isaac he was fettered,
in Jacob he was a hireling,
in Joseph he was sold,
in Moses he was exposed to die,
in David he was persecuted,
in the prophets he was scorned.

It is he who took flesh in the Virgin;
he was hung on the tree,
he was buried in the earth,
he was wakened from among the dead,
he was exalted to the heights of heaven.

He is the silent Lamb,
he is the Lamb slain,
who was born of Mary, the noble Lamb.

It is he who was taken from the flock
and led to sacrifice;
at evening he was sacrificed
and in the night he was buried;
he was not broken on the tree
and in the earth suffered no corruption;

he rose from the dead,
he rose from the depths of the tomb.

VII.

He was put to death. . . . Where was he put to death?
In the midst of Jerusalem. Why?

Because he had cured their lame,
because he had cleansed their lepers,
because he had restored sight to their blind,
because he had raised their dead.

That is why he suffered. Therefore it is written in the
Law and the prophets:

They returned me evil for good,
and my life has become barren.
They have plotted evil against me,
saying: "Let us load the just man with chains,
for he is a stumbling block to us."

O Israel, why have you committed this unheard-of
crime? You have dishonored him who honored you; you
have deprived of glory him who glorified you; you have
denied him who acknowledged you as his own; you have
rejected the proclamation of him who proclaimed you; you
put to death him who gave you life! Why did you do this,
O Israel? Was it not for you that it was written: "You shall
not shed innocent blood, lest you die a wretched death"?

"Yes," says Israel. "It is I who put the Lord to death."
"Why?"
"Because he had to suffer!"
"You are mistaken, Israel, when you make clever play
   of the Lord's sacrifice!

"He had to suffer,
      but not at your hands!
He had to be scorned,
      but not by you!"
He had to be judged,
      but not by you!
He had to be hanged on the cross,
      but not by you! . . .

"You were not moved to reverence for him
by the withered hand of the paralytic
that he made whole,
or by the eyes of the blind
that his hand reopened,
or by the bodies of the paralytics
that his voice restored to health.

You were not moved to fear
by this even stranger sign:
the dead man whom he called back from the tomb
where he had lain for four days.

"No, you took no account of these miracles, but in
order to immolate the Lord as evening came, you prepared
for him

      sharp nails
      and false witnesses
      and ropes and whips
      and vinegar and gall
      and sword and pain,
      as for a bandit who had shed blood.

"You scourged his body, you set upon his head a
crown of thorns, you bound his kindly hands that had
shaped you from the dust, you gave a drink of gall to the

noble mouth that had fed you with life, and you put your
Savior to death during the great feast!''

VIII.

Did you not know, O Israel,
that he is the firstborn of God,
begotten before the morning star?
He made the light shine
and the day be radiant. . . .

It is he who chose you
and led you on your road
from Adam to Noah,
from Noah to Abraham,
from Abraham to Isaac and Jacob
and to the twelve patriarchs.

It is he who guided you in Egypt
and protected you and fed you there.
It is he who lighted your way
with the column of fire
and who shaded you with the cloud.
He parted the Red Sea
and brought you across it
and scattered your enemies.

It is he who gave you the manna from heaven.
he gave you water from rock to drink,
gave you the Law on Horeb
and an inheritance on earth.
He sent you the prophets
and raised up your kings.

It is he who drew close to you,
who cared for the suffering in your midst
and raised the dead.

IX.

He has risen from the dead and cries:
Who will dispute with me?
Let him come before me!
It is I who have freed the condemned man,
it is I who gave life to the dead,
it is I who raised the buried!
What man shall gainsay me?

It is I, says Christ,
I who have destroyed death,
and triumphed over the enemy
and trodden hell under foot,
and chained the strong men,
and brought man to the heights of heaven:
It is I! says Christ.

Come then, all you races of men
whom sin has saturated,
and receive the forgiveness of sin.
For it is I who am your forgiveness,
I, the saving Pasch,
I, the Lamb sacrificed for you,
I, your purification, I, your life,
I, your resurrection, I, your light,
I, your salvation, I, your King!

It is I who bring you
to the heights of heaven;
it is I who shall raise you up here on earth.

I will show you the eternal Father,
I will raise you with my right hand!

X.

Such is he who made heaven and earth,
who in the beginning fashioned man,
who was foretold by the Law and the prophets,
who took flesh in the Virgin,

who was hanged on the tree,
who was buried in the earth,
who was awakened from among the dead,
who ascended to the heights of heaven,

who sits at the Father's right hand,
who has power to judge and save all men,
through whom the Father created all things
from the beginning to eternity!

He is the Alpha and the Omega,
he is the beginning and the end,
beginning that cannot be expressed
and end that is beyond our understanding!

He is the Christ,
he is the King,
he is Jesus,
the leader and the Lord!

He is risen from among the dead,
he sits at the Father's right hand,
he possesses the Father and is possessed by the Father.
To him be glory and power forever!
    Amen.

Melito, On the Pasch. —Peace to him who wrote this homily and to him who reads it and to those who love the Lord in simplicity of heart!

HOMILY ON THE PASCH, MELITO OF SARDIS

I.

Bridle of colts untamed,
  Over our wills presiding;
Wing of unwandering birds,
  Our flight securely guiding.
Rudder of youth unbending,
  Firm against adverse shock;
Shepherd, with wisdom tending
  Lambs of the royal flock:
Thy simple children bring
In one, that they may sing
In solemn lays
Their hymns of praise
With guileless lips to Christ their King.

II.

King of saints, almighty Word
Of the Father highest Lord;
Wisdom's head and chief;
Assuagement of all grief;
Lord of all time and space,
Jesus, Savior of our race;
Shepherd, who dost us keep;
  Husbandman, who tillest,

Bit to restrain us, Rudder
   To guide us as thou willest;
Of the all-holy flock celestial wing;
Fisher of men, whom thou to life dost bring;
   From evil sea of sin,
      And from the billowy strife,
   Gathering pure fishes in,
      Caught with sweet bait of life:
Lead us, Shepherd of the sheep,
   Reason-gifted, holy One;
King of youths, whom thou dost keep,
   So that they pollution shun:
Steps of Christ, celestial Way;
   Word eternal, Age unending;
Life that never can decay;
   Fount of mercy, virtue-sending;
Life august of those who raise
Unto God their hymn of praise,
      Jesus Christ!

III.

Nourished by the milk of heaven,
To our tender palates given;
Milk of wisdom from the breast
Of that bride of grace exprest;
By a dewy spirit filled
From fair Reason's breast distilled;
Let us sucklings join to raise
With pure lips our hymns of praise
As our grateful offering,
Clean and pure, to Christ our King.
Let us, with hearts undefiled,
Celebrate the mighty Child.
We, Christ-born, the choir of peace;

We, the people of his love,
Let us sing, nor ever cease,
To the God of peace above.

SAINT CLEMENT OF ALEXANDRIA

LET us receive the light
and we will receive God!
Let us receive the light
and become disciples of the Lord!
For he promised the Father:
"I will reveal your name to my brothers.
In the midst of the congregation I will sing of you."

Sing, O Word, his praises
and reveal God, your Father, to me!
Your words will save me
and your song will teach me.
Until now I was going astray
in search of God.
But ever since you enlightened me,
Lord, you have taught me to find
him who is my God as well,
and I receive your own Father from you.
I become his heir with you,
for you have not been ashamed of your brother.

CLEMENT OF ALEXANDRIA

Come, Janus; come, New Year; come, Sun, with strength renewed!

. . . .

soon to behold Ausonius enthroned in state, consul of Rome. What hast thou now beneath the Imperial dignity itself to marvel at? That famous Rome, that dwelling of Quirinus, and that Senate whose bordered robes glow with rich purple, from this point date their seasons in their deathless records.

Come, Janus; come, New Year; come, Sun, with strength renewed!

Year, that beginnest with good augury, give us in healthful Spring winds of sunny breath; when the Crab shows at the solstice, give us dews, and allay the hours of September with a cool north wind. Let shrewdly biting frosts lead in Autumn and let Summer wane and yield her place by slow degrees. Let the south winds moisten the seed corn, and Winter reign with all her snows until March, father of the old-style year, come back anew.

Come, Janus; come, New Year; come, Sun, with strength renewed!

Let May come back with new grace and fragrant breath of flowers, let July ripen crops and give the sea respite from eastern winds, let Sirius' flames not swell the heat of Leo's rage, let party-hued Pomona bring an array of luscious fruits, let Autumn mellow what Summer has matured, and let jolly Winter enjoy his portion due. Let the world live at peace, and no stars of trouble hold sway.

Come, Janus; come, New Year; come, Sun, with strength renewed!

Gradivus, let no star but such as favors thee invade thy house—not Cynthia, nor swift Arcas nearest to the earth, nor thou, O Saturn, moving remote in thy distant orbit: far from the Fiery Planet thou shalt move on thy peaceful course. Ye in conjunction move, star of health-bringing Jove, and Cytherean Vesper, nor ever let the Cyllenian, so complaisant to his guests, tarry far off.

Come, Janus; come, New Year; come, Sun, with strength renewed!

All foes now vanquished (where the mixed Frankish and Swabian hordes vie in submission, seeking to serve in our Roman armies; and where the wandering bands of Huns had made alliance with the Sarmatian; and where the Getae with their Alan friends used to attack the Danube—for Victory borne on swift wings gives me the news of this), lo now the Emperor comes to grace my dignity, and with his favor crowns the distinction which he would fain have shared.

Come, Janus; come, New Year; come, Sun, with strength renewed!

Offer thy golden joys, O Sun, to Janus, soon to come. A year, and Caesar shall succeed to the insignia of Ausonius, and wear for the fifth time the robe that distinguishes the Roman consul. Lo, how my honors are increased (hear this, O Nemesis, with an indulgent ear): Augustus deigns to appear as consul after me. It is as though he did more than rank me with himself now he has bidden me to bear the insignia before himself.

Come, Janus; come, New Year; come, Sun, with strength renewed!

Cause the one Tropic to give place to the Sun and again, make that other flee; that twice he (the Sun) may move through his changes from the Tropic Star and four times hasten to pass on from the three grouped signs. Urge on the Summer days, and let Caesar's promised year speed the Winter with its laggard nights. If I behold that year, then shall I be thrice, nay four times blessed; then shall I be doubly consul, then my head shall touch heaven itself.

AUSONIUS

ANTIPHON
My purity intact for you, my lamp alight in my hand,
Bridegroom, I come out to meet you.

Psalm 1
That cry from the heights, virgins,
could have wakened the dead.
"Out to the Bridegroom together," it said;
"take your lamps and white dresses;
make for the east.
Wake up, or else the King
will be indoors before you."

Antiphon
My purity intact for you, my lamp alight in my hand,
Bridegroom, I come out to meet you.

Psalm 2
Not for me the pale joys,
the pleasures, loves, of an existence
fed with mortal pleasure.
I long for you to take me in your arms
and give me life;
I want to look at you forever,
my Blessed One, my Beauty.

Antiphon
My purity intact for you, my lamp alight in my hand,
Bridegroom, I come out to meet you.

Psalm 3
Men offered me their beds: I scorned them;
scorned their houses too.
For you, my golden King,
I come in this fresh white dress.
I cannot wait to go inside that blissful place
and be with you.

Antiphon

> My purity intact for you, my lamp alight in my hand,
> Bridegroom, I come out to meet you.

Psalm 5

> I have forgotten the land I was born in,
> so deep your grace absorbs me, Word.
> I have no heart for friendly girls and dances,
> I no more care who my forebears were.
> You, Christ, you, are all in all to me.

Antiphon

> My purity intact for you, my lamp alight in my hand,
> Bridegroom, I come out to meet you.

Psalm 6

> Joy to you, Christ, Master of life's ballet,
> Light of our days, undimmed at evening.
> The virgins acclaim you; take what they bring you:
> Flower of all flowers, our Love, our Joy,
> Understanding, Wisdom, Word.

Antiphon

> My purity intact for you, my lamp alight in my hand,
> Bridegroom, I come out to meet you.

Psalm 7

> Stand by the open doors,
> queen in the glittering gown;
> bid us too welcome to the marriage room.
> Virgin your body, bride,
> splendid your victory,
> sweet the scent of your breath.
> See us now beside Christ,
> dressed like you, ready to celebrate
> your marriage, blest branch of God's olive.

Antiphon

>My purity intact for you, my lamp alight in my hand,
>Bridegroom, I come out to meet you.

Psalm 11

>Clear the colors Abel used
>to paint your death before you died,
>my Blessed.
>Down streamed his blood,
>his eyes sought heaven, as he said:
>"My brother's hand has made this cruel wound.
>Take me, Word, I beseech you."

Antiphon

>My purity intact for you, my lamp alight in my hand,
>Bridegroom, I come out to meet you.

Psalm 17

>John washed the crowds in the cleansing waters:
>you were to wash them too.
>A bad man sent him undeserved to death,
>for purity.
>Blood drenched the dust, but still he cried to you:

Antiphon

>My purity intact for you, my lamp alight in my hand,
>Bridegroom, I come out to meet you.

Psalm 18

>The mother, my Life, that bore you
>stood firm and fast in your grace.
>The womb that held you, spotless Germ,
>no man had sown with his seed.
>Virgin she was, though seeming to betray
>the marriage bed. Big with her blissful fruit she said:

Antiphon
> My purity intact for you, my lamp alight in my hand,
> Bridegroom, I come out to meet you.

Psalm 20
> We the bridesmaids
> sing your praises,
> happy woman, bride of God,
> virgin still, Ecclesia.
> Snow your body is, dark the waves of your hair,
> sound, unblemished, lovely creature.

Antiphon
> My purity intact for you, my lamp alight in my hand,
> Bridegroom, I come out to meet you.

Psalm 21
> Decay is destroyed; disease,
> with its pain and its tears, has gone.
> Death is no more, folly has fled
> and grief, that gnaws the mind,
> is dead. A sudden shaft of joy
> from Christ our God,
> and now this mortal world is shining.

Antiphon
> My purity intact for you, my lamp alight in my hand,
> Bridegroom, I come out to meet you.

Psalm 23
> So with a song that is new
> the band of virgins takes you up to heaven,
> bright queen.
> Wreathed with white lily-buds they go,
> the lamps in their hands ablaze with light.

Antiphon

> My purity intact for you, my lamp alight in my hand,
> Bridegroom, I come out to meet you.

Psalm 24

> Blest Father, beginning never,
> holding all things ever
> in strength together,
> taking the spotless heavens for your home:
> may we too pass beyond the gates of life,
> welcomed by you, O Father, and your Son.

Antiphon

> My purity intact for you, my lamp alight in my hand,
> Bridegroom, I come out to meet you.

METHODIUS OF OLYMPUS

LET us pray for peace, which is heaven's gift. May the
    Lord in his mercy give us peace.
Let us pray for faith. May the Lord give us grace to keep
    our faith in him untainted to the end.
Let us pray for unity of hearts and minds. May the Lord
    keep our minds and hearts as one.
Let us pray for patience. In all our afflictions may the Lord
    grant us patience to the end.
Let us pray for the apostles. May the Lord make us please
    him as they pleased him; may he fit us to receive the
    inheritance they have received.
Let us pray for the holy prophets. May the Lord add us to
    their number.
Let us pray for the holy confessors. The Lord grant that we
    may end our lives in the same frame of mind as they
    did.

Let us pray for the bishop. May our Lord grant him a long life and keep him true to the faith, that breaking the bread of truth as he ought, he may preside over the Church blamelessly and without reproach.

Let us pray for priests. May God not take the spirit of the priesthood from them, but grant them zeal and piety to the end.

Let us pray for deacons. The Lord grant that they may stay the course and attain holiness; and may he bear their labors and their charity in mind.

Let us pray for deaconesses. May the Lord answer their prayers and fill their hearts with all spiritual blessings and support them in their labors.

Let us pray for subdeacons and lectors. May the Lord give them patience and reward them for it.

Let us pray for the faithful throughout the world. The Lord grant that they may keep the faith whole and entire.

Let us pray for the empire. May the Lord grant it peace.

Let us pray for princes. The Lord grant that they may know him and fear him.

Let us pray for the whole world. May the Lord provide for all creatures and give to each what is best for it.

TESTAMENT OF OUR LORD JESUS CHRIST

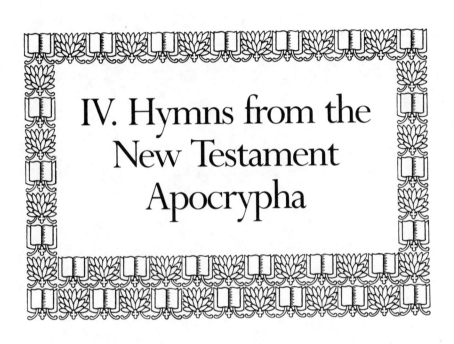

IV. Hymns from the New Testament Apocrypha

And when he had prayed and sat down,
he began to utter a psalm . . .

THE hymns in this chapter also date from the second
through the early fourth century, but they reflect a
different, far more heterodox, tradition of early Christianity. Even as certain groups of Christians in the first
century aligned themselves with Paul, Peter, or James of Jerusalem,
as Christianity spread throughout the Roman Empire other groups
identified with different apostles, such as Thomas, Andrew, and
John. Throughout Asia Minor, in places like Edessa and Antioch,
independent liturgical and literary traditions developed; the patron
apostle's legendary adventures and teachings were passed down
from generation to generation, then gathered in the books now
known as the New Testament Apocrypha. Exciting and colorful,
these books proved very popular. Today they not only serve as a
window on nonorthodox, often Gnostic, fashions of Christian
worship and belief, but many of them, for their imaginative
richness, both in language and theological lore, nurture the spirit as
well.

In part because hymns, through the license of poetry, are often
theologically more impressionic than homilies and tractates, some
hymns from the Apocrypha, such as that from the Acts of Peter,
and the first hymn from the Gospel of Bartholomew, would find a
comfortable home in more orthodox communions. In general,
however, they tend to be more ecstatic in nature, Gnostic in
theology (see the introduction to chapter 5), and less likely to be
tied to the confines of formal liturgy. For instance, following one's
personal prayers, one might burst into song as Thomas does, and
also Anna in the Protevangelium of James.

Among the more striking hymns here are those from the Acts
of Thomas. The first two are rhythmic invocations, which continue
an already established orthodox convention of evoking the divine
presence and stimulating communion with God by means of
repetitive chants. Repetition of the word "Come" may reflect the
primitive intonement of *Maranatha* ("Lord, come"), or "Thy

Kingdom come," both of which have eschatological force. The third hymn is a wedding hymn; one thinks of the marriage of Christ and the Church, a familiar motif in early Christian theology. The long and wonderful "Hymn of the Pearl" is a Gnostic hymn of redemption, recounting the tale of a lost soul who rediscovers his true identity and is reunited with his divine parents.

Other hymns, such as the selection from the Pseudo-Clementines and that from the Christian Sibyllines suggest the richness of these popular and poetic traditions of early Christian hymnody. Again, neither is overtly heterodox, and both have analogues in the Latin tradition.

The mesmerizing hymn from the Acts of John with which we close this section deserves special comment. This is a hymn of initiation into esoteric knowledge leading to salvation through liturgical dance ("He who does not dance / does not know what happens"). This esoteric dance, with its Gnostic hymnic accompaniment, directly transforms the participant into Christ.

COME, holy name of Christ that is above every name;
Come, power of the Most High and perfect compassion;
Come, thou highest gift;
Come, compassionate mother;
Come, fellowship of the male;
Come, thou that dost reveal the hidden mysteries;
Come, mother of the seven houses, that thy rest may be in
     the eighth house;
Come, elder of the five members, understanding, thought,
     prudence, consideration, reasoning,
Communicate with these young men!
Come, Holy Spirit, and purify their reins and their heart
And give them the added seal in the name of Father and
     Son and Holy Spirit.

ACTS OF THOMAS

COME, gift of the Most High;
Come, perfect compassion;
Come, fellowship of the male;
Come, Holy Spirit;
Come, thou that dost know the mysteries of the Chosen;
Come, thou that hast part in all the combats of the noble
     Athlete;

Come, treasure of glory;
Come, darling of the compassion of the Most High;
Come, silence
That dost reveal the great deeds of the whole greatness;
Come, thou that dost show forth the hidden things
And make the ineffable manifest;
Holy Dove
That bearest the twin young;
Come, hidden Mother;
Come, thou that art manifest in thy deeds and dost furnish
     joy
And rest for all that are joined with thee;
Come and partake with us in this Eucharist
Which we celebrate in thy name,
And in the love-feast
In which we are gathered together at thy call.

ACTS OF THOMAS

THE maiden is the daughter of light,
Upon her stands and rests the majestic effulgence of kings,
Delightful is the sight of her,
Radiant with shining beauty.
Her garments are like spring flowers,
And a scent of sweet fragrance is diffused from them.
In the crown of her head the king is established,
Feeding with his own ambrosia those who are set under
     him.
Truth rests upon her head,
By the movement of her feet she shows forth joy.
Her mouth is open, and that becomingly,
For with it she sings loud songs of praise.
Thirty and two are they that sing her praises.

Her tongue is like the curtain of the door,
Which is flung back for those who enter in.
Like steps her neck mounts up,
Which the first craftsman wrought.
Her two hands make signs and secret patterns, proclaiming
     the dance of the blessed aeons,
Her fingers open the gates of the city.
Her chamber is full of light,
Breathing a scent of balsam and all sweet herbs,
And giving out a sweet smell of myrrh and aromatic leaves.
Within are strewn myrtle branches and all manner of sweet-
     smelling flowers,
And the portals are adorned with reeds.
Her groomsmen keep her compassed about, whose number
     is seven,
Whom she herself has chosen;
And her bridesmaids are seven,
Who dance before her.
Twelve are they in number who serve before her
And are subject to her,
Having their gaze and look toward the bridegroom,
That by the sight of him they may be enlightened;
And forever shall they be with him in that eternal joy,
And they shall be at that marriage
For which the princes assemble together,
And shall linger over the feasting
Of which the eternal ones are accounted worthy,
And they shall put on royal robes
And be arrayed in splendid raiment,
And both shall be in joy and exultation
And they shall glorify the Father of all,
Whose proud light they received
And were enlightened by the vision of their Lord,
Whose ambrosial food they received,
Which has no deficiency at all,

And they drank too of his wine
Which gives them neither thirst nor desire;
And they glorified and praised, with the living Spirit,
The Father of Truth and the Mother of Wisdom.

ACTS OF THOMAS

"I praise thee, Jesus, that thou hast made me worthy not only of faith in thee, but also of suffering much for thy sake I thank thee therefore, Lord, that thou hast taken thought for me and given me patience. I thank thee, Lord, that for thy sake I have been called a sorcerer and a magician. May I therefore receive of the blessing of the humble, and of the rest of the weary, and of the blessings of those whom men hate and persecute and revile, speaking evil words of them. For lo, for thy sake am I hated; lo, for thy sake am I cut off from the many, and for thy sake they call me such as I am not!" And as he prayed all the prisoners looked at him, and besought him to pray for them. And when he had prayed and sat down, he began to utter a psalm in this fashion:

When I was a little child
And dwelt in my kingdom, the house of my father,
And enjoyed the wealth and the luxuries
Of those who brought me up,
From the East, our homeland,
My parents provisioned and sent me;
And from the wealth of our treasury
They had already bound up for me a load.
Great it was, but so light
That I could carry it alone:
Gold from Beth 'Ellaye

And silver from great Gazak
And chalcedonies of India
And opals of the realm of Kushan.
And they girded me with adamant,
Which crushes iron.
And they took off from me the splendid robe
Which in their love they had wrought for me,
And the purple toga,
Which was woven to the measure of my stature,
And they made with me a covenant
And wrote it in my heart, that I might not forget:
"If thou go down to Egypt
And bring the one pearl
Which is in the midst of the sea,
In the abode of the loud-breathing serpent,
Thou shalt put on again thy splendid robe
And thy toga which lies over it,
And with thy brother, our next in rank,
Thou shalt be heir in our kingdom."
I quitted the East and went down,
Led by two couriers,
For the way was dangerous and difficult
And I was very young to travel it.
I passed over the borders of Maisan,
The meeting place of the merchants of the East,
And reached the land of Babel,
And entered in to the walls of Sarbûg.
I went down into Egypt,
And my companions parted from me.
I went straight to the serpent,
Near by his abode I stayed,
Until he should slumber and sleep,
That I might take my pearl from him.
And since I was all alone
I was a stranger to my companions of my hostelry.
But one of my race I saw there,

A nobleman out of the East,
A youth fair and lovable,
An anointed one,
And he came and attached himself to me
And I made him my intimate friend,
My companion to whom I communicated my business.
I warned him against the Egyptians
And against consorting with the unclean.
But I clothed myself in garments like theirs,
That they might not suspect that I was come from without
To take the pearl,
And so might waken the serpent against me.
But from some cause or other
They perceived that I was not their countryman,
And they dealt with me treacherously
And gave me to eat of their food.
And I forgot that I was a king's son
And served their king.
And I forgot the pearl
For which my parents had sent me.
And because of the heaviness of their food
I fell into a deep sleep.
And all this that befell me
My parents observed and were grieved for me.
And a proclamation was published in our kingdom
That all should come to our gate,
The kings and chieftains of Parthia
And all the great ones of the East.
They made a resolve concerning me,
That I should not be left in Egypt,
And they wrote to me a letter
And every noble set his name thereto:
"From my father, the king of kings,
And thy mother, the mistress of the East,
And from thy brother, our other son,
To thee, our son in Egypt, greeting!

Awake and rise up from thy sleep,
And hearken to the words of our letter.
Remember that thou art a son of kings.
See the slavery—him whom thou dost serve!
Remember the pearl
For which thou didst journey into Egypt.
Remember thy splendid robe,
And think of thy glorious toga,
That thou mayest put them on and deck thyself therewith,
That thy name may be read in the book of the heroes
And thou with thy brother, our crown prince,
Be heir in our kingdom."
And the letter was a letter
Which the king had sealed with his right hand
Against the wicked, the people of Babel
And the rebellious demons of Sarbûg.
It flew in the form of an eagle,
The king of all birds,
It flew and alighted beside me
And became all speech.
At its voice and the sound of its rustling
I awoke and stood up from my sleep,
I took it and kissed it,
Broke its seal and read.
And even as it was engraven in my heart
Were the words of my letter written.
I remembered that I was a son of kings
And my noble birth asserted itself.
I remembered the pearl
For which I was sent to Egypt,
And I began to cast a spell
On the terrible loud-breathing serpent.
I brought him to slumber and sleep
By naming my father's name over him,
And the name of our next in rank
And of my mother, the queen of the East.

And I snatched away the pearl
And turned about, to go to my father's house.
And their dirty and unclean garment
I took off and left in their land,
And directed my way that I might come
To the light of our homeland, the East.
And my letter, my awakener,
I found before me on the way;
As with its voice it had awakened me,
So it led me further with its light,
Written on Chinese tissue with ruddle,
Gleaming before me with its aspect
And with its voice and its guidance
Encouraging me to speed,
And drawing me with its love.
I went forth, passed through Sarbûg,
Left Babel on my left hand
And came to the great city Maisan,
The haven of the merchants,
Which lies on the shore of the sea.
And my splendid robe which I had taken off,
And my toga with which it was wrapped about,
From the heights of Warkan Hyrcania
My parents sent thither
By the hand of their treasurers,
Who for their faithfulness were trusted therewith.
Indeed I remembered no more its dignity,
For I had left it in my childhood in my father's house,
But suddenly, when I saw it over against me,
The splendid robe became like me, as my reflection in a
         mirror;
I saw it wholly in me,
And in it I saw myself quite apart from myself,
So that we were two in distinction
And again one in a single form.
And the treasurers too

Who had brought it to me, I saw in like manner,
That they were two of a single form,
For one sign of the king was impressed upon them,
His who restored to me through them
The honor, my pledge, and my riches,
My splendid robe adorned
Gleaming in glorious colors,
With gold and beryls,
Chalcedonies and opals,
And sardonyxes of varied color,
This also made ready in its grandeur,
And with stones of adamant
Were all its seams fastened.
And the likeness of the king of kings
Was completely embroidered all over it
And like stones of sapphire again in its
Grandeur resplendent with manifold hues.
And again I saw that all over it
The motions of knowledge were stirring.
And I saw too
That it was preparing as for speech.
I heard the sound of its songs
Which it whispered at its descent:
"I belong to the most valiant servant,
For whom they reared me before my father,
And I perceived also in myself
That my stature grew according to his labors."
And with its royal movements
It poured itself entirely toward me,
And in the hands of its bringers
It hastened, that I might take it;
And my love also spurred me
To run to meet it and receive it,
And I stretched out and took it.
With the beauty of its colors I adorned myself.
And my toga of brilliant colors

I drew completely over myself.
I clothed myself with it and mounted up
To the gate of greeting and homage.
I bowed my head and worshiped
The spendor of the father who had sent it to me,
Whose commands I had accomplished,
As he also had done what he promised.
And at the gate of his satraps
I mingled among his great ones.
For he rejoiced over me and received me,
And I was with him in his kingdom.
And with the sound of the organ
All his servants praise him.
And he promised me that to the gate
Of the king of kings I should journey with him again
And with my gift and my pearl
With him appear before our king.

HYMN OF THE PEARL, ACTS OF THOMAS

HAIL, O cross; indeed may you rejoice. I know well that
you will rest in the future because for a long time you have
been weary set up awaiting me. I am come to you whom I
recognize as mine own; I am come to you, who long for
me. I know the mystery for which you have indeed been
set up. For you are set up in the cosmos to establish the
unstable. And one part of you stretches up to heaven so
that you may point out the heavenly Logos, the head of all
things. Another part of you is stretched out to right and left
that you may put to flight the fearful and inimical power
and draw the cosmos into unity. And another part of you is
set on the earth, rooted in the depths, that you may bring
what is on earth and under the earth into contact with what

is in heaven. O Cross, tool of salvation of the Most High! O Cross, trophy of the victory of Christ over his enemies! O Cross, planted on earth and bearing your fruit in heaven! O name of the Cross, filled with all things! Well done, O Cross, that you have bound the circumference of the world! Well done, form of understanding, that you have given a form to your own formlessness! Well done, invisible discipline, that you discipline severely the substance of the knowledge of many gods and drive out from humanity its discoverer! Well done, O Cross, that you have clothed yourself with the Lord, and borne as fruit the robber, and called the apostle to repentance, and not thought it beneath you to receive us! But for how long shall I say these things and not be embraced by the cross, that in the cross I may be made to live and through the cross I may go out of this life into the common to all death? Approach, ministers of my joy and servants of Aegeates, and fulfill the desire we both have and bind the lamb to the suffering, the man to the Creator, the soul to the Savior.

ACTS OF ANDREW

HE beareth our sins and is afflicted for us; yet we thought him to be afflicted and stricken with wounds. For he is the Father and the Father in him; he also is himself the fullness of all majesty, who has shown us all his goodness. He ate and drank for our sakes, though himself without hunger or thirst, he bore and suffered reproaches for our sakes, he died and rose again because of us. He who defended me also when I sinned and strengthened me with his greatness, will also comfort you that you may love him, this God who is both great and little, beautiful and ugly, young and old, appearing in time and yet in eternity wholly invisible;

whom no human hand has grasped, yet is held by his servants, whom no flesh has seen, yet now he is seen; whom no hearing has found, yet now he is known as the word that is heard; whom no suffering can reach, yet now is chastened as we are; who was never chastened, yet now is chastened; who is before the world, yet now is comprehended in time; the beginning greater than all princedom, yet now delivered to the princes; beauteous, yet appearing among us as poor and ugly, yet foreseeing; this Jesus you have, brethren, the door, the light, the way, the bread, the water, the life, the resurrection, the refreshment, the pearl, the treasure, the seed, the abundance, the mustard seed, the vine, the plough, the grace, the faith, the word: He is all things, and there is no other greater than he. To him be praise for ever and ever. Amen.

ACTS OF PETER

GLORY be to thee, O Lord Jesus Christ,
who givest to all thy grace which we have all perceived.
Alleluia.
Glory be to thee, O Lord, the life of sinners.
Glory be to thee, O Lord, through whom death is put to
    shame.
Glory be to thee, O Lord, the treasure of righteousness.
We praise thee as God.

THE GOSPEL OF BARTHOLOMEW

O womb more spacious than a city!
O womb wider than the span of heaven!
O womb that contained him whom the seven heavens do
    not contain.
You contained him without pain
and held in your bosom him who changed his being into
    the smallest of things.
O womb that bare, concealed in your body,
the Christ who has been made visible to many.
O womb that became more spacious than the whole
    creation.

THE GOSPEL OF BARTHOLOMEW

And Anna sighed toward heaven, and saw a nest of
sparrows in the laurel tree and immediately she made
lamentation within herself:

"Woe to me, who begot me,
What womb brought me forth?
For I was born as a curse before them all and before the
    children of Israel,
And I was reproached, and they mocked me and thrust me
    out of the temple of the Lord.

Woe is me, to what am I likened?
I am not likened to the birds of the heaven;
for even the birds of the heaven are fruitful before thee, O
    Lord.
Woe is me, to what am I likened?
I am not likened to the unreasoning animals;
for even the unreasoning animals are fruitful before thee, O
    Lord.

Woe is to me, to what am I likened?
I am not likened to the beasts of the earth;
for even the beasts of the earth are fruitful before thee, O
      Lord.

Woe is me, to what am I likened?
I am not likened to these waters;
for even these waters gush forth merrily, and their fish
      praise thee, O Lord.
Woe is me, to what am I likened?
I am not likened to this earth;
for even this earth brings forth its fruit in its season and
      praises thee, O Lord."

THE PROEVANGELIUM OF JAMES

RULER and Lord of all,
Father and God,
guard thou the shepherd with the flock.

Thou art the cause,
Thou art the power.
We are that for which help is intended.
Thou art the helper,
the physician,
the savior,
the wall,
the life,
the hope,
the refuge,
the joy,
the expectation,
the rest;
in a word: Thou art everything.

Help, deliver, and preserve us
unto eternal salvation.
Thou canst do all things.
Thou art the Sovereign of sovereigns,
the Lord of lords,
the Ruler of kings.

Give thou power to the president to loose what is to be
      loosed
and to bind what is to be bound.
Through him as thine instrument
preserve the church of thy Christ as a beautiful bride.
For thine is eternal glory.

Praise to the Father
and to the Son
and to the Holy Spirit
to all eternity. Amen.

THE PSEUDO-CLEMENTINES

Mary's virginity and her giving birth escaped the notice of
the prince of this world, as did the Lord's death—those
three secrets dying to be told, but wrought in God's
silence. How, then, were they revealed to the ages?

A star shone in heaven
brighter than all the stars.

Its light was indescribable
and its novelty caused amazement.

The rest of the stars,
along with the sun and the moon,
formed a ring around it.

Yet it outshone them all and there was bewilderment
whence this unique novelty had arisen.

As a result all magic lost its power
and all witchcraft ceased.

Ignorance was done away with,
and the ancient kingdom of evil was utterly destroyed.

For God was revealing himself as a man,
to bring newness of eternal life.

What God had prepared was now beginning.
Hence everything was in confusion
as the destruction of death was being taken in hand.

EPHESIANS 19, IGNATIUS OF ANTIOCH

I sing from the heart the great son and famous of the
     Immortal,
To whom the Most High, his begetter, gave a throne
     to take
Ere he was born; for according to the flesh he was raised up
The second time, after he had washed in the stream of the
     river
Jordan, which is borne along on silvery foot, drawing its
     waves.
Who first, escaping from fire, shall see God

Coming in sweet spirit, on the white wings of a dove.
And a pure flower shall blossom, and springs gush forth.
He shall show ways to men, he shall show heavenly paths;
And he shall teach all with wise speeches.
He shall bring to judgment and persuade a disobedient
      people,
Proudly declaring the praiseworthy race of his heavenly
      Father.
He shall walk the waves, and deliver men from sickness,
He shall raise up the dead, and banish many pains.
And from one wallet there shall be sufficiency of
      bread for men
When David's house puts forth its shoot. In his hand
Is all the world, and earth and heaven and sea.
He shall flash like lightning on the earth, as at his first
      appearance
Two saw him, begotten from each other's side.
It shall be, when earth shall rejoice in the hope of
    a Son.
   But for thee alone, land of Sodom, evil woe lies waiting;
For thou in thy folly didst not perceive thy God
When he came in the eyes of men. But from the thorn
Thou didst weave a crown, and bitter gall didst thou
      mingle
For an insulting drink. This will bring thee evil woe.
   O tree most blessed, on which God was stretched out,
Earth shall not have thee, but thou shalt see a heavenly
      home,
When thy fiery eye, O God, shall flash like lightning.

                                  CHRISTIAN SIBYLLINES

PRAISED is, and praised may he be,
the dear son of Love,
the life-giver Jesus,
the chief of all these gifts.
Praised is and praised shall be the Virgin of Light,
the chief of all excellences.
Praised is and praised shall be the holy religion
through the power of the Father,
through the blessing of the Mother
and through the goodness of the Son.
Salvation and blessing upon the sons of salvation
and upon the speakers and the hearers of the renowned
        word!
Praise and glory be to the Father
and to the Son
and to the elect Breath, the Holy Spirit,
and to the creative elements!
The word of the "living gospel" of the eye and ear is
        taught,
and the fruit of truth is presented.
The Blessed shall receive this offering . . . ;
the wise shall know;
the strong shall put on good things to him that
        knoweth . . . .
For all is,
and all that is and shall be exists through his power.

THE GOSPEL OF MANI

'GLORY be to thee, Father.'
And we circled round him and answered him, 'Amen.'
        'Glory be to thee, Logos:
            Glory be to thee, Grace,'—'Amen.'
        'Glory be to thee, Spirit:

Glory be to thee, Holy One:
  Glory be to thy Glory.'—'Amen.'
'We praise thee, Father:
  We thank thee, Light:
    In whom darkness dwelleth not.'—'Amen.'
'And why we give thanks, I tell you:
  'I will be saved,
    And I will save.'—'Amen.'
  'I will be loosed,
    And I will loose.'—'Amen.'
  'I will be wounded,
    And I will wound.'—'Amen.'
  'I will be born,
    And I will bear.'—'Amen.'
  'I will eat,
    And I will be eaten.'—'Amen.'
  'I will hear,
    And I will be heard.'—'Amen.'
  'I will be thought,
    Being wholly thought.'—'Amen.'
  'I will be washed,
    And I will wash.'—'Amen.'

Grace dances.
  'I will pipe,
    Dance, all of you.'—'Amen.'
  'I will mourn,
    Beat you all your breasts.'—'Amen.'
  'The one Ogdoad
    sings praises with us.'—'Amen.'
  'The twelfth number
    dances on high.'—'Amen.'
  'To the Universe
    belongs the dancer.'—'Amen.'
  'He who does not dance
    does not know what happens.'—'Amen.'

'I will flee,
   and I will remain.'—'Amen.'
'I will adorn,
   and I will be adorned.'—'Amen.'
'I will be united,
   and I will unite.'—'Amen.'
'I have no house,
   and I have houses.'—'Amen.'
'I have no place,
   and I have places.'—'Amen.'
'I have no temple
   and I have temples.'—'Amen.'
'I am a lamp to you
   who see me.'—'Amen.'
'I am a mirror to you
   who know me.'—'Amen.'
'I am a door to you
   who knock on me.'—'Amen.'
'I am a way to you
   the traveler.'—'Amen.'
'Now if you follow
   my dance,
see yourself
   in Me who am speaking,
and when you have seen what I do,
   keep silence about my mysteries.
You who dance, consider
   what I do, for yours is
This passion of man
   which I am to suffer.
For you could by no means
   have understood what you suffer
unless to you as Logos
   I had been sent by the Father.
You who saw what I suffer
   saw me as suffering,

and seeing it you did not stay
  but were wholly moved.
Being moved toward wisdom
  you have me as a support;
    rest in me.
Who I am, you shall know
  when I go forth.
What I now am seen to be,
  that I am not;
What I am you shall see
  when you come yourself.
If you knew how to suffer
  you would be able not to suffer.
Learn how to suffer
  and you shall be able not to suffer.
What you do not know
  I myself will teach you.
I am your God,
  not the God of the traitor.
I will that there be prepared
  holy souls for me.
Understand the word
  of wisdom!
As for me,
  if you would understand what I was:
By the word I mocked at all things
  and I was not mocked at all,
I exulted:
  but do you understand the whole,
and when you have understood it, say,
  Glory be to thee, Father.

'Say again with me,
    Glory be to thee, Father,
      Glory be to thee, Word.
        Glory be to thee, Spirit.'—'Amen.'

ACTS OF JOHN

V. Gnostic Hymns
from Nag Hammadi

I give thanks by singing a hymn to thee.
For I have received life from thee
when thou madest me wise.

THE DISCOURSE ON THE EIGHTH AND NINTH

WITH the exception of the first and last selections in this chapter, all the hymns included here are taken from the Nag Hammadi library, a collection of predominently Gnostic Coptic Christian writings unearthed in the sands of Egypt in 1945. The first selection, a Gnostic psalm recorded by Hippolytus in his *Refutation of all Heresies,* unfolds the history of salvation from a radically different perspective than parallel Christian hymns contained in chapter 2. The last selection, an otherwise orthodox hymn contained in the Gnostic *Corpus Hermeticum,* demonstrates how various traditions of early Christian hymnody coexisted with one another.

Gnostic Christianity replaces faith with knowledge (or *gnosis*). Salvation lies in cracking the cosmic code and thereby discovering one's true identity. Here Christ is not a savior so much as he is a messenger, sent to awaken his divine brothers and sisters to their own divinity, that they may rejoin him in the heavenly realm. With the remembrance of one's divine origin, and an understanding of the condition into which one has fallen, one gains power over the devil and the archons, the death-keepers, who would detain in their prison of death-bound matter all who remain in this life ignorant of their true nature. Thus ignorance is death, and self-knowledge the key to redemption.

In the Discourse on the Eighth and Ninth we see the emphasis on calling the sacred (hidden) name common in Gnostic works. Knowing the proper names of the various powers is salvifically significant. The calling here of chanted nonsense vowels is indicative, perhaps, of speaking in tongues. Ancient magical traditions are the religious environments in which these types of hymns and chants evolved.

The hymn from the First Apocalypse of James, a composition intended as a hymnic vehicle for saving knowledge, is an excellent example of the theologically creative potential of early Christian hymns. That from the Second Apocalypse, a direct response to orthodox claims, shows how hymns might be developed for polemical purposes ("For you are not the redeemer," etc.).

Hymns of philosophical transport, such as those from the Tripartite Tractate, are characteristic of the more orthodox neo-Platonic tradition of the Greek East. In such instances, a hymn is the medium for theological reflection in the *via negativa* mode to the ineffable, invisible, incomprehensible one.

The Three Steles of Seth, offering elaborate and poetic incantations to a triple power in what might be called a revelatory ascent, translate orthodox triadology to Gnostic sectarian teachings by replacing the Holy Spirit with a god beyond God. In the first, the sect's traditional revealer, Emmacha Seth, leads the praise to his father Geradamas, perhaps a Christ-like figure; in the second, the congregational chorus praises the first aeon in their ascent to the invisible Father; and, in the third, they are in the presence of the inconceivable One, the Father of Divinity. Here again, as with the dance in the Acts of John, the experience of chanting revelatory hymns of ascent is salvific in itself.

THE world's producing law was primal Mind,
And next was Firstborn's outpoured Chaos;
And third, the soul received its law of toil:
Encircled, therefore, with an aqueous form
With care o'erpowered it succumbs to death.
Now holding sway, it eyes the light,
And now it weeps on misery flung;
Now it mourns, now it thrills with joy;
Now it wails, now it hears its doom;
Now it hears its doom, now it dies,
And now it leaves us, never to return.
It, hapless straying, treads the maze of ills.
But Jesus said, Father, behold,
A strife of ills across the earth
Wanders from thy breath of wrath;
But bitter Chaos seeks to shun,
And knows not how to pass it through.
On this account, O Father, send me;
Bearing seals, I shall descend;
Through ages whole I'll sweep,
All mysteries I'll unravel,
And forms of Gods I'll show;
And secrets of the saintly path,
Styled "Gnosis," I'll impart.

PSALM OF THE NAASSENES

I give thanks by singing a hymn to thee. For I have
received life from thee when thou madest me wise. I praise
thee. I call thy name that is hidden within me: a ō ee ō ēēē
ōōō iii ōōōō ooooo ōōō ōō uuuuuu ōō ōōōōōōōōō
ōōōōōōōōō ōō. Thou are the one who exists with the
spirit. I sing a hymn to thee reverently.

THE DISCOURSE ON THE EIGHTH AND NINTH

YOU have come with knowledge,
that you might rebuke their forgetfulness.
You have come with recollection,
that you might rebuke their ignorance.

For you descended into a great ignorance,
but you have not been defiled by anything in it.
For you descended into a great mindlessness,
and your recollection remained.

You walked in mud,
and your garments were not soiled,
and you have not been buried in their filth,
and you have not been caught.

THE FIRST APOCALYPSE OF JAMES

FOR you are not the redeemer
nor a helper of strangers.
You are an illuminator and a redeemer
   of those who are mine,
and now of those who are yours.
You shall reveal to them;
you shall bring good among them all.

You admire
   because of every powerful deed.
You are he whom the heavens bless.
You he shall envy,
   he who has called himself your Lord.
I am the [. . .]
   those who are instructed in these
      things with you.

For your sake
   they will be told these things,
   and will come to rest.
For your sake
   they will reign,
   and will become kings.
For your sake
   they will have pity
   on whomever they pity.

For just as you are first
   having clothed yourself,
you are also the first who will strip himself,
and you shall become as you were
   before you were stripped.

THE SECOND APOCALYPSE OF JAMES

I.

He is of such kind and such form and such great magnitude
　　that no one else has been with him from the beginning;
　　nor is there a place in which he is, or from which he has
　　　　come forth, or into which he will go;
　　nor is there a primordial form which he uses as a model
　　　　in his work;
　　nor is there any difficulty which accompanies him in
　　　　what he does;
　　nor is there any material set out for him, from which he
　　　　creates what he creates;
　　nor any substance within him from which he begets what
　　　　he begets;
　　nor a coworker who, along with him, does what he
　　　　does.

II.

Nor can any work express him,
nor can any eye see him,
nor can any body grasp him,
　　because of his inscrutable greatness,
　　and his incomprehensible depth,
　　and his immeasurable height,
　　and his illimitable will.

III.

He is sustenance;
he is joy;
he is truth;
he is rejoicing;
he is rest.
That which he conceives,
that which he sees,
that about which he speaks,

the thought which he has,
    transcends all wisdom,
    and is above all intellect,
    and is above all glory,
    and is above all honor,
        and all sweetness,
        and all greatness,
        and any depth,
        and any height.

IV.

He himself,
    since in the proper sense he begets himself as ineffable
        one,
    since he is self-begotten,
    since he conceives of himself,
    and since he knows himself as he is,
        namely as the one who is worthy of his admiration,
        and glory, and honor, and praise,
    since he produces himself
        because of the boundlessness of his greatness,
        and the unsearchability of his wisdom,
        and the immeasurability of his power,
        and his untasteable sweetness,
he is the one who projects himself in this manner of
generation, thus having honor and a wondrous glory of
love; the one who gives himself glory, who wonders, who
honors, who also loves; the one who has a Son,
    who subsists in him,
    who is silent concerning him;
    who is the ineffable one in the ineffable one,
    the invisible one,
    the incomprehensible one,
    the inconceivable one in the inconceivable one.

THE TRIPARTITE TRACTATE

I bless thee, Father, Geradamas, I, as thine own Son, Emmacha Seth, whom thou didst beget unconceived, as a blessing of our God; for I am thine own Son. And thou art my mind, O my Father. And I, I sowed and begot; but thou hast seen the majesties. Thou hast stood, being unceasing. I bless thee, Father. Bless me, Father. It is because of thee that I exist; it is because of God that thou dost exist. Because of thee I am with that very one. Thou art light, since thou beholdest light. Thou hast revealed light. Thou art Mirotheas; thou art my Mirotheos. I bless thee as God; I bless thy divinity. Great is the good self-begotten who stood, the God who was first to stand. Thou didst come in goodness; thou hast appeared, and thou hast revealed goodness. I shall utter thy name, for thou art a first name. Thou art unconceived. Thou hast appeared in order that thou mightest reveal the eternal ones. Thou art he who is. Therefore thou hast revealed those who really are. Thou art he who is uttered by a voice, but by mind art thou glorified, thou who hast dominion everywhere. Therefore the perceptible world too knows thee because of thee and thy seed. Thou art merciful.

And thou art from another race, and its place is over another race. And now thou art from another race, and its place is over another race. Thou art from another race, for thou art not similar. And thou art merciful, for thou art eternal. And thy place is over a race, for thou hast caused all these to increase, though because of my seed. For it is thou who knows it, that its place is in begetting. But they are from other races, for they are not similar. But their place is over other races, for their place is in life. Thou art Mirotheos.

I bless his power which was given to me, who caused the malenesses that really are to become male three times, who was divided into the pentad, the one who was given

to us in triple power, the one who was begotten
unconceived, the one who came from what is select;
because of what is humble, he went forth in the midst.

Thou art a Father through a Father, a word from a
command. We bless thee, Thrice Male, for thou didst unite
the all through them all, for thou hast empowered us. Thou
hast come from one through one; thou hast moved, thou
hast come to one. Thou hast saved, thou hast saved, thou
hast saved us, O crown-bearer, crown-giver! We bless thee
eternally. We bless thee, once we have been saved, as the
perfect individuals, perfect on account of thee, those who
became perfect with thee who is complete, who completes,
the one perfect through all these, who is similar
everywhere, Thrice Male.

Thou hast stood. Thou wast first to stand. Thou wast
divided everywhere. Thou didst continue being one. And
those whom thou hast willed, thou hast saved. But thou
dost will to be saved all who are worthy.

Thou art perfect! Thou art perfect! Thou art perfect!

THE FIRST STELE OF SETH

GREAT is the first aeon, male virginal Barbelo, the first
glory of the invisible Father, he who is called "perfect."

Thou hast seen first him who really preexists, that he is
nonbeing. And from him and through him thou hast
preexisted eternally, the nonbeing from one indivisible,
triple power, thou a triple power, thou a great monad from
a pure monad, thou an elect monad, the first shadow of the
holy Father, light from light.

We bless thee, producer of perfection, aeon-giver. Thou hast seen the eternal ones, that they are from a shadow. And thou hast become numerable. And thou didst find, thou didst continue being one; yet becoming numerable in division, thou art threefold. Thou art truly thrice, thou one of the one. And thou art from a shadow of him, thou a Hidden One, thou a world of understanding, knowing those of the one, that they are from a shadow. And these are thine in the heart.

For their sake thou has empowered the eternals in being; thou hast empowered divinity in living; thou hast empowered knowledge in goodness; in blessedness thou hast empowered the shadows which pour from the one. Thou hast empowered this one in knowing; thou hast empowered another one in creating. Thou hast empowered him who is equal and him who is not equal, him who is similar and him who is not similar. Thou hast empowered in begetting, and provided forms in that which is to others. . . . Thou hast empowered these.—He is that One Hidden in the heart.—And thou hast come forth to these and from these. Thou art divided among them. And thou dost become a great male First-Appearer.

Fatherly God, divine child, begetter of multiplicity according to a division of all who really are, thou hast appeared to them all in a word. And thou dost possess them all unconceived and eternally indestructible on account of thee.

Salvation has come to us; from thee is salvation. Thou art wisdom, thou knowledge; thou art truthfulness. On account of thee is life; from thee is life. On account of thee is mind; from thee is mind. Thou art a mind, thou a world of truthfulness, thou a triple power, thou threefold. Truly thou art thrice, the aeon of aeons. It is thou only who sees purely the first eternal ones and the unconceived ones.

But the first divisions are as thou wast divided. Unite us as thou has been united. Teach us those things which thou dost see. Empower us that we may be saved to eternal life. For we are each a shadow of thee as thou art a shadow of that first preexistent one. Hear us first. We are eternal ones. Hear us as the perfect individuals. Thou art the aeon of aeons, the all-perfect one who is established.

Thou hast heard! Thou hast heard!

Thou hast saved! Thou hast saved!

We give thanks! We bless always! We shall glorify thee!

THE SECOND STELE OF SETH

WE rejoice! We rejoice! We Rejoice!

We have seen! We have seen! We have seen the really preexistent one really existing, being the first eternal one.

O Unconceived, from thee are the eternal ones and the aeons, the all-perfect ones who are established, and the perfect individuals.

We bless thee, nonbeing, existence which is before existences, first being which is before beings, Father of divinity and life, creator of mind, giver of good, giver of blessedness!

We all bless thee, knower, in a humble blessing, thou because of whom all these are. . . . really, . . . , who knows thee through thee alone. For there is no one who is active before thee. Thou art an only and living spirit. And thou knowest one, for this one who belongs to thee is on every side. We are not able to express him. For thy light shines upon us.

Present a command to us to see thee, so that we may be saved. Knowledge of thee, it is the salvation of us all. Present a command! When thou dost command, we have been saved! Truly we have been saved! We have seen thee by mind! Thou art them all, for thou dost save them all, he who was not saved, nor was he saved through them. For thou, thou hast commanded us.

Thou art one, thou art one, just as there is one who will say to thee: Thou art one, thou art a single living spirit. How shall we give thee a name? We do not have it. For thou art the existence of them all. Thou art the life of them all. Thou art the mind of them all. For thou art he in whom they all rejoice.

Thou hast commanded all these to be saved through thy word . . . glory who is before him, Hidden One, blessed Senaon, he who begat himself, Asineus, . . . Ephneus, Optaon, Elemaon the great power, Emouniar, Nibareus, Kandephoros, Aphredon, Deiphaneus, thou who art Armedon to me, power-begetter, Thalanatheus, Antitheus, thou who existeth within thyself, thou who art before thyself—and after thee no one entered into activity.

As what shall we bless thee? We are not empowered. But we give thanks, as being humble toward thee. For thou hast commanded us, as he who is elect, to glorify thee to the extent that we are able. We bless thee, for we were saved. Always we glorify thee. For this reason we shall glorify thee, that we may be saved to eternal salvation. We have blessed thee, for we are empowered. We have been saved, for thou hast willed always that we all do this.

We all did this. . . . not through . . . aeon. . . . , the one who was . . . , we and those who . . . He who will remember these and give glory always will become perfect among those who are perfect and unattainable from any quarter. For they all bless these individually and together. And afterwards they shall be silent. And just as they were ordained, they ascend. After the silence, they descend. From the third they bless the second; after these the first. The way of ascent is the way of descent.

Know therefore, as those who live, that you have attained. And you taught yourselves the infinite things. Marvel at the truth which is within them, and at the revelation.

THE THIRD STELE OF SETH

HOLY is God the Father of all, who is before the first
        beginning;
holy is God, whose purpose is accomplished by his several
        powers;
holy is God, who wills to be known, and is known by
        them that are his own.
    Holy art thou, who by thy word hast constructed all
        that is;
holy art thou, whose brightness nature has not darkened;
holy art thou, of whom all nature is an image.
    Holy art thou, who art stronger than all domination;
holy art thou, who art greater than all preeminence;
holy art thou, who surpassest all praises.
    Accept pure offerings of speech from a soul and heart
        uplifted
to thee, thou of whom no words can tell, no tongue can
        speak,
whom silence only can declare.

CORPUS HERMETICUM

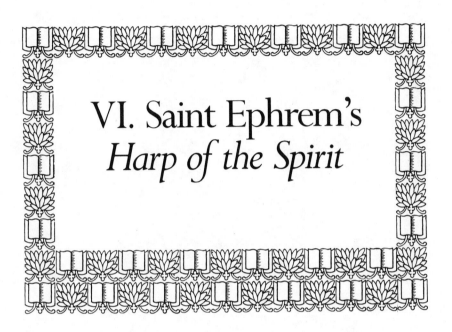

VI. Saint Ephrem's
Harp of the Spirit

This joyful festival is entirely made up
    of tongues and voices:
innocent young women and men
    sounding like trumpets and horns.

HYMNS ON THE RESURRECTION 2

W ITH the possible exceptions of Clement of Alexandria and Saint Gregory Nazianzus, no Christian poet invested early Christian hymnody with more eloquence than a little-known fourth-century theologian from Edessa, Saint Ephrem. He wrote his verses in Syriac, a dialect of Aramaic, the language Jesus spoke. Writing before Syriac literature had been pervaded by the influence of Hellenistic traditions, his hymns formally reflect ancient Semitic patterns—parallel structure and antithesis—familiar to readers of the Jewish scriptures, and subtly woven into the paradoxical thought patterns so favored by Jesus.

Enlisting choirs of women to sing them at worship, Saint Ephrem composed hymns that might best be described as the first anthems. Though he also wrote prose homilies, meant to be recited not sung, his hymns have a didactic or homiletic quality about them as well. Through analogy and metaphor, he utilized them as vehicles for theological reflection and instruction: as in the Hymn of Faith 73, a hymn not of praise but of problem solving, in which he proposes a resolution to the paradox of the trinity; and, in the Hymn of Faith 82, in which he indulges in constructive theological reflection and teaching by elaborating upon the Sign of Jonah.

As with his homilies, Saint Ephrem offered not only theological instruction but also pastoral comfort in certain of his hymns. Examples of this latter approach are his Nisibene Hymn 52, a dialogue between Death and Satan, and the Hymn on the Resurrection 2. In both cases, the heart of his offering is one of consolation and moral edification for people struggling with the reality of death.

Edessa was a center for heterodox activity, and Saint Ephrem employed his hymns as a corrective of what he considered to be popular misconceptions of Christian theology. But he was far from being a literalist, as his interpretations of well-known scriptural passages clearly indicate. He approached the Bible symbolically, always honoring its mystery while employing poetic license to develop analogies that might help to illumine that mystery and strengthen our faith.

I have invited you, Lord, to a wedding feast of song,
but the wine—the utterance of praise—at our feast has
      failed.
You are the guest who filled the jars with good wine,
fill my mouth with your praise.

The wine that was in the jars was akin and related to
this eloquent wine that gives birth to praise
seeing that that wine too gave birth to praise
from those who drank it and beheld the wonder.

You who are so just, if at a wedding feast not your own
you filled six jars with good wine,
do you, at this wedding feast, fill, not the jars,
but the ten thousand ears with its sweetness.

Jesus, you were invited to the wedding feast of others,
here is your own pure and fair wedding feast: gladden your
      rejuvenated people,
for your guests too, O Lord, need
your songs; let your harp utter!

The soul is your bridal chamber,
your guests are the senses and the thoughts.
And if a single body is a wedding feast for you,
how great is your banquet for the whole church!

The holy Moses took the synagogue up on Sinai;
he made her body shine with garments of white, but her
        heart was dark;
she played the harlot with the calf, she despised the Exalted
        one,
and so he broke the tablets, the book of her covenant.

Who has ever seen the turmoil and insult
of a bride who played false in her own bridal chamber,
        raising her voice?
When she dwelt in Egypt she learnt it from
the mistress of Joseph, who cried out and played false.

The light of the pillar of fire and of the cloud
drew into itself its rays
like the sun that was eclipsed
on the day she cried out, demanding the King, a further
        crime.

How can my harp, O Lord, ever rest from your praise?
How could I ever teach my tongue infidelity?
Your love has given confidence to my shamefacedness,
—yet my will is ungrateful.

It is right that man should acknowledge your divinity,
it is right for heavenly beings to worship your humanity;
the heavenly beings were amazed to see how small you
        became,
and earthly ones to see how exalted!

Refrain: Praise to you from all who perceive your truth.

HYMNS ON FAITH, 14

TAKE as symbols   of the Father the sun,
of the Son the light,   and of the Holy Spirit
the warmth.

Being one,   yet therein is to be seen
a trinity;   who can explain
what lies beyond comprehension?

The one is multiple: the one consists of three,
and the three constitute one,   a great astonishment,
a manifest wonder.

The sun is distinct   from its radiance,
yet mingled with it,   for its radiance
is also the sun.

Yet none speak   of two suns,
though its radiance   is also a sun
to those down below.

Nor do we speak   of two Gods.
our Lord   being also God
over creation.

Who can probe   how or where
the sun's ray is attached,   its warmth attached,
yet each is free?

Neither are they quite separate,   nor indeed confused:
distinct, yet commingled, attached, yet each is free—
a great wonder.

Can anyone spy out   and grope after them—
things apparently   so simple
and straightforward?

Spy out the sun for me,   separate from its radiance;
look for and identify separately   its warmth,
if you can.

Distinguish the sun   from its radiance,
and the warmth   from both of these,
if you are able.

The sun   is on high,
while its heat and light   are with those below—
a manifest symbol.

Its radiance   has bent down to earth
where it rests in the eye,   having clothed itself
as though with a body.

When the eye is closed   in sleep,
then the ray strips it off   like a dead body
that will be raised up again.

How the light   gets into the eye
no one understands—just as with our Lord
who dwelt in the womb.

The light put on,   from within the eye,
a fair appearance,   then it goes forth
and visits the created world,

—Just as our Savior,   who put on the body
in all its frailty,   and then went forth to sanctify
the whole of creation.

But when the ray   returns back
to its source,   never having been parted
from its begetter.

It leaves here   its warmth,
just like the Holy Spirit, whom our Lord
left with his disciples.

Consider the analogies   in the created world,
and do not be in doubt   about the threefold persons,
otherwise you will find yourself lost:

What was difficult for you   I have now made clear:
how the One consists of Three,   yet this Trinity
is a single Essence.

Refrain: Blessed is he who sent you.

HYMNS OF FAITH, 73

WHAT is it you resemble? Let your silence
        speak
to one who listens to you; with silent mouth
speak with us, for to him who hears
the whisper of your silence
your symbol proclaims in silence our Savior.

Your mother is the virgin bride of the sea
—without its having married her; she fell into its bosom
—without its being aware; she conceived you in it
—though it knew her not. Your symbol
rebukes the Jewish girls when they wear you.

You of all gems are the only one
whose begetting resembles that of the Word of the Most
        High,
whom, in unique fashion,
the Most High begot, while other engraved gems
symbolically resemble those things created on high.

O visible offspring of a hidden womb!
O mighty symbol, your pure conception
required no seed; your chaste birth needed
no intercourse; you have no brothers
for your birth is unique.

Our Lord has brothers—and yet he has none,
for he is the Only-begotten. O solitary pearl,
great is the mystery, for your symbol
stands all alone, yet on the royal crown
you have brethren and sisters!

The fair gems shall be your brothers,
along with the beryls; and other pearls
are as your companions, while gold shall be,
as it were, your relative: the King of kings shall have
a crown constituted out of your dear friends.

When you came up from the depths of the sea
—the living grave—you acquired this
glorious band of brethren, relatives
and kinsmen. As wheat on the stalk,
so are you on the diadem, set amongst many.

As a debt is justly
returned to you, so you are raised from that depth
to the glorious height. The stalk in the field
bears the wheat: you the king's head,
as though a chariot, carries about.

O daughter of the waters, who left the sea
in which you were born, you went up to the dry land
in which you were cherished. Men cherished you, seized
          you
and were adorned with you: so too with the Child
whom the gentiles cherished, being crowned with him.

In symbol and in truth Leviathan is trodden down
by mortals: the baptized, like divers, strip
and put on oil, as a symbol of Christ
they snatched you and came up: stripped,
they seized the soul from his embittered mouth.

Your nature resembles the Silent Lamb
with his gentleness: even though a man pierce it,
takes it and hangs it on his ear,
as it were on Golgotha, all the more does it throw out
its bright rays on those who behold it!

In your beauty is the Son's beauty depicted:
—the Son who clothed himself in suffering, nails went
        through him.
Through you the awl passed, you too did they pierce,
as they did his hands. But because he suffered he reigns
—just as your beauty is increased through your suffering.

If they had spared you, then they would not have cherished
        you,
for, if you have suffered, you now reign. Simon Peter
had pity on the Rock by which all who struck it
were wounded. It is because of his suffering
that his beauty now adorns both height and depth.

HYMNS ON FAITH, 82

WHILE I live I will give praise, and not be as
        if I had no existence;
I will give praise during my lifetime, and will not be a dead
        man among the living.
For the man who stands idle is doubly dead,
the earth that fails to produce defrauds him who tills it.

In you, Lord, may my mouth give forth praise out of
      silence.
Let not our mouths be barren of praise,
let not our lips be destitute of confession;
may the praise of you vibrate within us!

Those who are themselves fashioned of dust fashion dust,
      and the earthborn labor on the earth.
We love our bodies, which are akin to us, of the same
      origin:
for our roots are dust
and our branches bear the fruits of our works.

"Take no care for today"—yet we are busy caring for years
      ahead.
He who clothes all reproves those who weave with the
      example of the lilies,
He who sustains all and gives all things to all men
rebukes the greedy with the greedy crows.

Our generation is like a leaf whose time, once it falls is
      over,
but though the limit of our life is short, praise can lengthen
      it,
for, corresponding to the extent of our love,
we shall acquire, through praise, life that has no measure.

For it is in our Lord that the root of our faith is grafted:
though far off, he is still close to us in the fusion of love.
Let the roots of our love be bound up in him.
Let the full extent of his compassion be fused in us.

O Lord, may the body be a temple for him who built it,
may the soul be a palace full of praise for its architect!
Let not our body become a hollow cavity,
let our souls not be a harbor of loss.

And when the light of this temporal breath flickers out
do you relight in the morning the lantern that was
          extinguished in the night.
The sun arrives and with the warmth of its rising
it revives the frozen and relights what has been
          extinguished.

It is right that we should acknowledge that Light which
          illumines all,
for in the morning, when the sun has gone up, lanterns are
          extinguished,
but this new Sun has performed a new deed,
relighting in Sheol the lanterns that had been extinguished.

In place of death who has breathed the smell of mortality
          over all,
he who gives life to all exhales a life-giving scent in Sheol
from his life the dead breathe in new life,
and death lies within them.

The scent of the buried Elisha who gave life to a dead man
          provides a type for this:
a man dead but a day breathed in life from him who was
          long dead;
the life-giving scent wafted from his bones and entered the
          dead corpse
—a symbol of him who gives life to all.

Jesus has elucidated for us the symbols that took place at
          Elisha's grave.
how from an extinguished lantern a lantern can be relit,
and how, while lying in the grave he could raise up the
          fallen,
himself remaining there, but sending forth a witness to
          Christ's coming.

However much, Lord, I would feel you, it is still not you
        yourself I touch,
for my mind can touch nothing of your hiddenness:
it is just a visible, illuminated, image
that I see in the symbol of you: for all investigation into
        your being is hidden.

Refrain: In you, Lord, may my mouth bear the fruit of
        praise that is acceptable to you.

NISIBENE HYMNS, 50

I heard Death and Satan loudly disputing
which was the strongest of the two amongst men.

Death has shown his power in that he conquers all men.
Satan has shown his guile in that he makes all men sin.

Death: Only those who want to, O Evil One, listen to
            you,
            but to me they come, whether they will or not.

Satan: You just employ brute force, O Death,
            whereas I use traps and cunning snares.

Death: Listen, Evil One, a cunning man can break
            your yoke,
            but there is none who can escape from mine.

Satan: You, Death, exercise your strength on the sick,
            but I am the stronger with those who are well.

Death: The Evil One has no control over the person
who reviles him,
but all who have cursed me, in the past or
now, still come to me.

Satan: You, Death, received your power from God,
but when I make men sin I do it without any
outside help.

Death: You, Evil One, lay snares like a coward,
but I use my power like a king.

Satan: You are too stupid, Death, to recognize how
great I am,
seeing that I can capture free will.

Death: You, Evil One, go around like a hooligan,
whereas I am like a lion, fearlessly crushing my
prey.

Satan: You have no one who serves or worships you,
O Death,
but me kings honor with sacrifices, like a god.

Death: But many address Death as a benefactor,
whereas no one ever has or shall call on you as
such, O Evil One.

Satan: Do you not realize, Death, how many
call on me in one way or another, and offer me
libations?

Death: Your name is hated, Satan,
you cannot remedy it; everyone curses your
name. Hide your shame.

Satan: Your ear is dull, Death, for you fail to hear
            how everyone howls out against you. Go, hide
                yourself.

Death: I go open-faced among creation, and do not use
                deceit like you:
            you do not pass a single night without some
                kind of deceit.

Satan: You have not found a better lot for all your
                truth:
            men hate you just as much as they do me.

Death: Everyone fears me as a master.
            but you they hate as the Evil One.

Satan: People hate your name and your deeds. O
                Death:
            my name may be hated, but my pleasures are
                loved.

Death: Your sweet taste ends in setting the teeth on
                edge;
            remorse always accompanies those pleasures of
                yours.

Satan: Sheol is hated for there is no chance of remorse
                there:
            it is a pit which swallows up and suppresses
                every impulse.

Death: Sheol is a whirlpool, and everyone who falls in
                it is resurrected,
            but sin is hated because it cuts off a man's
                hope.

Satan: Although it grieves me, I allow for repentance;
           you cut off a sinner's hopes if he dies in his
               sins.

Death: With you his hope was cut off long ago;
           if you had never made him sin, he would have
               made a good end.

Chorus: Blessed is he who set the accursed slaves against
           each other
           so that we can laugh at them just as they
               laughed at us.

           Our laughing at them now, my brethren, is a
               pledge
           that we shall again be enabled to laugh, at the
               resurrection.

Refrain: Praise to you, Son of the Shepherd of all, who
           has saved his flock
           from the hidden wolves, the Evil One and
               Death, who had swallowed it up.

NISIBENE HYMNS, 52

YOUR law has been my vessel
   revealing to me something of Paradise.
Your Cross has been to me the key
   which opened up this Paradise.
From the Garden of Delights did I gather
   and carry back with me from Paradise
roses and other eloquent blooms
   which are here scattered about for your feast

amid songs as they flutter down on humanity.
  Blessed is he who both gave and received the crown!

This joyful festival is entirely made up
  of tongues and voices:
innocent young women and men
  sounding like trumpets and horns,
while infant girls and boys
  resemble harps and lyres;
their voices intertwine
  as they reach up together toward heaven,
giving glory to the Lord of glory.
  Blessed is he for whom the silent have thundered out.

The earth thunders out below,
  heaven above roars with thunder:
Nisan has mingled together the two sounds—
  of those above and those below.
The shouts from the holy Church
  are joined with the Divinity's thunder,
and with the bright torches
  lightning flashes mingle in,
with the rain came the tears of sorrow,
  with the pasturage, the Paschal fast.

It was in similar wise
  that in the Ark all voices cried out:
outside the Ark were fearsome waves.
  but inside, lovely voices;
tongues, all in pairs,
  uttered together in chaste fashion,
thus serving as a type of our festival now
  when unmarried girls and boys
sing together in innocence
  praise to the Lord of that Ark.

At this festival when each person offers
  his fine actions as offerings,
I lament, dear Lord,
  that I stand here so impoverished.
But my mind grows green again with your dew:
  for it a second Nisan is come,
whose flowers serve as my offerings,
  garlanded in all kinds of wreathes,
laid at the door of each ear!
  Blessed is the Cloud which has distilled in me its
    moisture!

Who has ever beheld blossoms
  gathered from the Scriptures, as though it were from the
    hills?
With them has every young girl
  filled the spacious bosom of her mind.
The voice of song, like the sun, has scattered
  blossoms all over the crowds:
these flowers are sacred,
  catch them with your senses,
just as our Lord caught Mary's unguent.
  Blessed is he who is garlanded with his handmaids!

Fair and eloquent flowers
  have the children strewn before the King:
the donkey was garlanded with them,
  the path was filled with them;
they scattered praises like flowers,
  their songs of joy like lilies.
Now too at this festival
  does the crowd of children scatter for you, Lord,
halleluias like blossoms.
  Blessed is he who was acclaimed by young children.

It is as though our hearing embraced
    an armful of children's voices,
while chaste songs, Lord,
    fill the bosoms of our ears.
Let each of us gather up a posy of such flowers,
    and with these let each intersperse
blossoms from his own piece of land,
    so that, for this great feast,
we may plait a great garland.
    Blessed is he who invited us to plait it!

Let the chief pastor weave together
    his homilies like flowers,
let the priests make a garland of their ministry,
    the deacons of their reading,
strong young men of their jubilant shouts,
    children of their psalms,
virgins of their songs,
    chief citizens of their benefactions
ordinary folk of their manner of life.
    Blessed is he who gave us so many opportunities for
      good!

Let us summon and invite the saints,
    the martyrs, apostles and prophets,
whose own blossoms and flowers
    shine out like themselves—
such a wealth of roses they have,
    so fragrant are their lilies:
from the Garden of Delights do they pluck them,
    and they bring back fair bunches
to crown our beautiful feast.
    O praise to you from the saints who are blessed.

Royal crowns appear poor
    compared with the wealth of your crown

into which purity is intertwined,
   in which faith shines out,
humility shines forth,
   and holiness is commingled
and great love is resplendent.
   O great King of all flowers,
how perfect is the beauty of your crown.
   Blessed is he who gave it us to weave!

Receive our offering, O our King,
   and in return grant us salvation;
give peace to the land that has been devastated,
   rebuild the churches that were burnt,
so that when deep peace has returned
   we may plait you a great wreath,
with flowers and people to plait it,
   coming in from all sides
so that the Lord of peace may be crowned.
   Blessed is he who has acted and is able to act.

HYMNS OF THE RESURRECTION, 2

O God of mercies, who didst refresh Noah, he too refreshed thy mercies. He offered sacrifices and stayed the flood: he presented gifts and received the promise. With prayer and incense, he propitiated thee: with an oath and with the bow, thou wast gracious to him; so that if the flood should essay to hurt the earth, the bow should stretch itself over against it, to banish it away, and hearten the earth. As thou hast sworn peace, so do thou maintain it, and let they bow strive against thy wrath.

   Stretch forth thy bow against the flood, for lo!
   it has lifted up its waves against our walls!

In revelation, Lord, it has been proclaimed that that lowly blood which Noah sprinkled wholly restrained thy wrath for all generations: how much mightier, then, shall be the blood of thy Only-Begotten, that the sprinkling of it should restrain our flood! For lo! it was but as mysteries of him that those lowly sacrifices gained virtue, which Noah offered, and stayed by them thy wrath. Be propitiated by the gift upon my altar, and stay from me the deadly flood. So shall both thy signs bring deliverance: to me thy cross, and to Noah thy bow. Thy cross shall cleave the sea of waters: thy bow shall stay the flood of rain.

> *Stretch forth thy bow against the flood, for lo!*
> *it has lifted up its waves against our walls!*

Lo! all the billows trouble me, and thou hast given more favor to the Ark: waves alone encompassed it; mounds and weapons and waves encircle me. It was unto thee a storehouse of treasures, but I have been a storehouse of debts. It, in thy love, subdued the waves: I, in thy wrath am left desolate among the weapons. The flood bore it: the river threatens me. O Helmsman of that Ark: Be my Pilot on the dry land! To it, thou gavest rest in the haven of a mountain: to me, also, give thou rest in the haven of my walls!

> *Stretch forth thy bow against the flood, for lo!*
> *it has lifted up its waves against our walls!*

The Just One has chastened me abundantly, but it he loved, even among the waves. For Noah overcame the waves of lust, which had drowned in his generation the sons of Seth. Because his flesh revolted against the daughters of Cain, his chariot rode on the surface of the waves. Because women defiled him not, he coupled the beasts, whereof in the Ark he joined together all pairs in the yoke of wedlock. The olive, which with its oil gladdens the face, with its leaf gladdened their countenances: for me the river whereof to drink is wont to make joyful, lo! O Lord, by its flood it makes me mournful.

> *Stretch forth thy bow against the flood, for lo!*
> *it has lifted up its waves against our walls!*

O Lord: gladden thou in me the imprisoned ones of my fortresses, thou who didst gladden those in the Ark with the olive leaf! Thou sentest healing by means of the dove to the sick ones that were drowning in every war; it entered in, and drove out all their pains. For the joy of it swallowed up all their sorrows, and mourning vanished away in its consolation. And as the chief of a host gives heartening to the fugitives, so the dove disseminated courage among the forsaken. Their eyes tasted the sight of peace, and their mouths hasted to open in thy praise. As the olive leaf in the waves, save thou me, that thou mayest gladden in me the prisoners of my fortresses.

> *Stretch forth thy bow against the flood, for lo!*
> *it has lifted up its waves against our walls!*

The flood assails, and dashes against our walls: may the all-sustaining might uphold them! It falls not as the building on the sand, for I have not built my doctrine upon the sand: a rock shall be for me the foundation, for on thy rock have I built my faith: the secret foundation of my trust shall support my walls. For the walls of Jericho fell, because on the sand she had built her trust. Moses built a wall in the sea, for on a rock his understanding built it. The foundation of Noah was on a rock: the dwelling place of wood it bore up in the sea.

> *Stretch forth thy bow against the flood, for lo!*
> *it has lifted up its waves against our walls!*

Compare the souls which are in me with the living things that were in the Ark; and instead of Noah who mourned in it, lo!—thy altar mourning and humbled. Instead of the

wedded wives that were in it, lo! my virgins that are
unmarried. Instead of Ham who went forth from it, and
uncovered his father's nakedness, lo! workers of
righteousness who have nourished and clothed apostles. In
my pains, O my Lord, I rave in my speech: blame me not
if my words provoke thee! Thou puttest to silence the
prosperous when they murmured: have mercy on me as on
them that were silenced aforetime!

> *Stretch forth thy bow against the flood, for lo!*
> *it has lifted up its waves against our walls!*

Before thy wrath, thou madest a house of refuge, and all
the nations rebelled against it. Noah was refreshed in rest,
that his dwelling place should give rest according to his
name. Thou didst close the doors to save the righteous one:
thou didst open the doors to destroy the unclean. Noah
stood between the terrible waves that were without and the
destroying mouths that were within: the waves tossed him
and the mouths dismayed him. Thou madest peace for him
with them that were within: thou broughtest down before
him them that were without: thou didst speedily change his
troubles, for light to thee, O Lord, are hard things.

> *Stretch forth thy bow against the flood, for lo!*
> *it has lifted up its waves against our walls!*

Hear and weigh the comparison of me with Noah, and
though my suffering be light beside his, let thy mercy make
our deliverance alike: for lo! my children stand like him,
between the wrathful and the destroyer. Give peace, O
Lord, among them that are within and humble before me
them that are without, and give me twofold victory! And
whereas the slayer has made his rage threefold, may he of
the three days show me threefold mercy! Let not the Evil
One overcome thy loving kindness: seeing he has assailed
me twice, and thrice overcome thou him! Let my victory
fly abroad through the world, that it may earn thee praise

in the world! O thou who didst rise on the third day: give us not over to death in our third peril!

> *Stretch forth thy bow*
> *Against the flood, for lo!*
> *It has lifted up its waves*
> *Against our walls!*

> *Kyrie, eleison.*
> *Kyrie, eleison.*
> *Kyrie, eleison.*

> *Christe, eleison.*
> *Christe, eleison.*
> *Christe, eleison.*

> *Kyrie, eleison.*
> *Kyrie, eleison.*
> *Kyrie, eleison. Amen.*

HYMNS FOR A TIME OF TRIBULATION

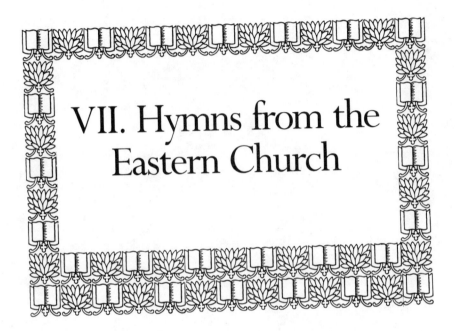

VII. Hymns from the
Eastern Church

I sing your praises, O Father,
Healer of hearts,
Healer of bodies.

SYNESIUS

B Y the middle of the fourth century, both in the east and
in the west, not only had Christianity become established as the state religion, but the liturgy, including its
various hymnic elements, had taken the shape it would
hold for centuries. We include the most important liturgies,
especially eucharistic liturgies, in *The Macmillan Book of Earliest
Christian Prayers,* but have selected a few examples here that
demonstrate how hymns, especially in the form of chanted litanies,
have by this time also been institutionalized as instruments of
ecclesiastical intercession (for example, Gregory Nazianzus's prayer
for general well-being, which closes this chapter). Noteworthy also
is the emergence of saints, first and most prominently the Virgin
Mary, as proper objects of hymnic praise (as in the Invocations of
the Blessed Virgin by Saint John Chrysostom and Saint Basil, and
the Saint Cyril of Alexandria's appeal for the Virgin's intercession).

Another characteristic that distinguishes especially eastern
hymnody is its ascetic character, showing the profound influence
of the development of eastern monastic life. Synesius's hymn, with
which we open, is a prayer for purity, as are several of the hymns of
Saint Gregory Nazianzus. These latter demonstrate the way in
which morning and evening hymns were now being employed in
personal devotions, both for preparation at the beginning of the
day, and for confession or thanksgiving at day's end.

To underscore the intimate relationship between established
hymnic patterns and the credal formulae that in the fourth century
begin to emerge from the great Church councils, we also include in
this chapter the creed of Saint Athanasius, and a small exerpt from
the statement of faith by Athanasius's principle theological oppo-
nent, Arius. In their utilization of parallel structure and repetitive
elaboration, not only are such faith statements reminiscent of one
prominent strain of early Christian hymnody (going back as far as

the prologue to the Gospel of John), but they also emerge from the liturgy itself (cf. The Apostles' Creed) and are directly influenced by hymnodic patterns. This is yet another indication of the close relationship between the profession of credal orthodoxy and the singing of the mass.

WHEN the dawn appears,
When the light grows,
When midday burns,
When has ceased
The holy light,
When the clear night comes;
I sing your praises, O Father,
Healer of hearts,
Healer of bodies,
Giver of wisdom,
Remedy of evil,
O Giver also
Of a life without evil,
A life not troubled
By earthly fear—
Mother of distress,
Mother of sorrows—
Keep my heart
In purity,
Let my songs speak
Of the hidden source
Of created things;
And, far from God,
Never let me drawn
Into sin.

SYNESIUS

I.

Thou, Blessed Bride of God,
The Good Earth whence,
For the world's salvation,
Sprang the ear untilled,
Account me worthy,
Eating thereof, to be saved!

II.

Most holy table of the Bread of Life,
Which, to show mercy, from above
Came down and new life giveth
To the world:
Suffer me, though unworthy, now in fear,
To taste thereof, and live!

III.

Lady: Propitiate the Child of thy womb for me:
Preserve thy servant pure and undefiled,
That I may gain the mystical Pearl,
And so be sanctified!

IV.

O Mary,
Mother of God!
Thou, honored dwelling place
Of a sweet odor:
Make by thy prayers of me
A chosen vessel to receive
The hallowing of thy Son!

V.

At the entreaty of thy holy Mother,
Hallow me altogether,
O sacred word of God and God,
As to thy divine mysteries nigh I draw:
Amen.

VI.

Favored of God,
Beyond all understanding,
Thou didst bring forth
Christ, the Savior!

I, thy defiled servant,
Now beseech thee, undefiled:
Cleanse me from all defilement
Of flesh and spirit,
For now I seek to draw nigh
To the most pure mysteries!

VII.

From thy pure blood did God take flesh:
Wherefore, O Lady,
Every generation calls thee blessed,
And multitudes of bodiless Spirits
Do glory in glorifying thee,
For they behold through thee, with open gaze,
Him who over all things beareth rule,
In human nature manifest!

VIII.

Great
Is the multitude of my transgressions,
Mother of God!

Unto thy purity I have recourse,
Seeking salvation.
Visit my soul in my infirmity,
And pray thy Son, our God,
To grant me remission of my evil deeds
Thou,
Who alone art blessed!

SAINT JOHN CHRYSOSTOM AND SAINT BASIL

I.

O Blessed Mother of God:
Open the gate of compassion
To us whose hope is in thee,
That we may not be confounded,
But be preserved from adversity, through thee,
Who art the salvation of Christian folk.

II.

O thou who art
A well of tenderness,
Vouchsafe unto us thy compassion,
Mother of God!

Look down upon thy people
Who have sinned,
And show thy pardon as of old:

For in thee do we put our trust
And hail thee blessed
As once did Gabriel,
Chief captain of the bodiless hosts.

III.

It is very meet to bless thee
Who didst bring forth God,
Ever blessed and most spotless
And the Mother of our God.
More honorable than cherubim,
And more than the seraphim
Glorious incomparably, thou,
Who, inviolate, didst bring forth God the Word,
And art indeed Mother of God:
Thee
Do we magnify!

O Full of Grace!
Thou art the joy of all creation,
Of the assembly of the angels
And the race of men—
Thou, hallowed temple,
Spiritual Paradise,
And boast of maidenhood, whence God took Flesh,
When he, who was before the worlds our God,
Became a child.

Thy womb he made his throne,
And he enlarged thy bosom
Broader than the heavens.

O Full of Grace!
Thou art the joy of all creation.
Glory be to thee!

IV.

Arise! shine,
O new Jerusalem!
For the glory of the Lord is risen upon thee!
Now rejoice and be glad,
O city of Zion:
Appear in thy splendor,
Pure Mother of God,
For he whom thou barest is risen!

O thou, great Passover,
And hallowed above all,
O Christ!
O thou the Wisdom and the Word,
The power of God!
Grant that we may partake of thee
More truly,
In that day of thy kingdom
Which shall have no night!

V.

Steadfast Protectress of Christians,
Constant Advocate with the Creator,
Disdain not the cry of the sinful,
But of thy goodness,
Be ready to succor us,
Who do call with all confidence to thee:

Make haste to hear our petition.
Make hast to supplicate for us,
O Mother of God,
Who ever didst protect them that pay honor to thee!

VI.

More honorable than cherubim,
And more than seraphim incomparably glorious,
Thou, who, inviolate,
Forth didst bring God the Word,
And art indeed Mother of God:
Thee do we magnify!

Glory be to the Father
And to the Son,
And to the Holy Ghost,
Both now, and forever,
Henceforth eternally: Amen.

SAINT JOHN CHRYSOSTOM AND SAINT BASIL

BLESSED be the kingdom of the Father, the Son, and the Holy Ghost, now and forever, world without end: Amen.

In time of peace, let us pray to the Lord:

Lord: Have mercy on us.

For the peace from on high, and for the salvation of our souls, let us pray to the Lord:

Lord: Have mercy on us.

For the peace of the whole world, for the good estate of all the holy Churches of God, and for the unity of all, let us pray to the Lord:

Lord: Have mercy on us.

For this holy house and for those who enter therein with faith, reverence, and fear of God, let us pray to the Lord:

Lord: Have mercy on us.

For our most holy pope, and our God-beloved bishops, for the venerable order of priests, for religious and deacons of Christ, for all the clergy and people, let us pray to the Lord:

Lord: Have mercy on us.

Let us pray for mercy, life, peace, health, salvation, protection, forgiveness, and remissions of sins to the servants of God, the dwellers in this place:

Lord: Have mercy on us.

For our most pious and God-protected sovereigns, for all their court and families, let us pray to the Lord:

Lord: Have mercy on us.

Let us pray for the blessed and ever memorable benefactors of this Church, and for all our brethren and fathers departed who rest in peace near this place, and for all the orthodox throughout the world:

Lord: Have mercy on us.

Let us pray for those who offer fruits and who do good in this holy and most venerable Church, for the workmen, singers, and all the people here present who await from God great and rich mercy:

Lord: Have mercy on us.

For this realm, and for every city and country, and for all the faithful who dwell therein, let us pray to the Lord:

Lord: Have mercy on us.

For a good state of climate, abundance of the fruits of the earth, and peaceful seasons, let us pray to the Lord:

Lord: Have mercy on us.

For sailors, travelers, the sick, sufferers, prisoners, for the salvation of all, let us pray to the Lord:

Lord: Have mercy on us.

That we may be delivered from all affliction, wrath, peril, and necessity, let us pray to the Lord:

Lord: Have mercy on us.

Help, save, pity, and guard us, O God, by thy grace:

Lord: Have mercy on us.

Remembering our all-holy, immaculate, most worshipful and glorious Lady, the Mother of God and ever-virgin Mary, and all the saints, let us commend ourselves, each other, and all our life to Christ our God:

Lord Jesus Christ: Have mercy on us.

Lord Almighty, God of our fathers: We pray thee hear and have mercy on us:

Have mercy on us, O God, according to thy great mercy.

We pray thee: Hear and have mercy on us. Help, save, pity, and guard us, O God, by thy grace:

Lord: Have mercy on us.

That this whole day be perfect, holy, peaceful, and sinless, let us ask the Lord:

Grant, O Lord!

For an Angel of peace, a faithful guide and guardian of our souls and bodies let us ask the Lord:

Grant, O Lord!

For pardon and forgiveness of our sins and offenses, let us ask the Lord:

Grant, O Lord!

For what is good and profitable to our souls, and for peace in the world, let us ask the Lord:

Grant, O Lord!

That our God send us his divine grace and the gifts of the Holy Ghost, let us ask the Lord:

Grant, O Lord!

That the rest of our lives be spent in peace and repentance, let us ask the Lord:

Grant, O Lord!

For a Christian end to our lives, without pain or blame, and peaceful, and for a defense at his dread Tribunal, let us ask the Lord:

Grant, O Lord!

Having prayed for union of faith and communion of the Holy Ghost, let us commend ourselves, each other, and our whole life to Christ our God.

Let us love one another, that we may with one mind confess Father, Son, and Holy Ghost, the consubstantial and undivided Trinity.

And may the mercies of our great God and Savior Jesus Christ be with us all:

Sanctus Sanctus Sanctus:
Amen

SAINT JOHN CHRYSOSTOM

HAIL, O Mary, Mother of God,
Virgin and Mother!
Morning Star, perfect vessel.

Hail, O Mary, Mother of God!
Holy Temple
in which God himself was conceived.

Hail, O Mary, Mother of God!
chaste
and pure dove.

Hail, O Mary, Mother of God!
effulgent light, from thee
proceedeth the Sun of Justice.

Hail, O Mary, Mother of God!
Thou didst enclose in thy sacred womb
the One who cannot be encompassed.

Hail, O Mary, Mother of God!
With the shepherds we sing
the praise of God;
with the angels, the song of thanksgiving,

> *Glory to God in the highest*
> *and peace on earth*
> *to men of goodwill!*

Hail, O Mary, Mother of God!
from thee flowed the True Light,
Jesus Christ,
our Lord.

Hail, O Mary, Mother of God!
through thee came to us the Conqueror
and triumphant Vanquisher of hell.

Hail, O Mary, Mother of God!
through thee blossoms the glory of the Resurrection.

Hail, O Mary, Mother of God!
Thou hast saved every faithful Christian.

Hail, O Mary, Mother of God!
Who can praise thee worthily,
O glorious Virgin Mary?

> *Holy Mary, Mother of God,*
> *pray for us sinners*
> *now and at the hour of our death. Amen.*

SAINT CYRIL OF ALEXANDRIA

WHOSOEVER will be saved, before all things, it is necessary to hold the Catholic faith, which, except every man keep whole and inviolate, without doubt he shall perish everlastingly. And the Catholic faith is this:

That we worship one God in Trinity in Unity, neither confounding the Persons, nor dividing the Substance.

For there is one Person of the Father, another of the Son, another of the Holy Ghost.

But the Godhead of the Father, and of the Son, and of the Holy Ghost is but one, the glory equal, and the Majesty coeternal.

Such as the Father is, such is the Son, and such is the Holy Ghost:

The Father uncreated,
The Son uncreated,
The Holy Ghost uncreated;
The Father infinite,
The Son infinite,
The Holy Ghost infinite;
The Father eternal,
The Son eternal,
And the Holy Ghost eternal.

Yet there are not three eternals, but one Eternal. And so
there are not three uncreated, nor three infinite, but one
Uncreated and one Infinite.

So also the Father is almighty, the Son almighty, and the
Holy Ghost almighty.

—Yet there are not three almighties, but one Almighty.

So the Father is God, the Son is God, and the Holy Ghost
is God.

—Yet there are not three gods, but one God.

So the Father is Lord, the Son is Lord, and the Holy
Ghost is Lord.

—Yet there are not three lords, but one Lord.

For, as we are compelled by the Christian faith to
acknowledge each Person by himself to be God and Lord:
so we are forbidden by the Catholic religion to say that
there are three gods or three lords.

The Father is made of none, neither created nor begotten.
The Son is of the Father alone, not made, nor created, but
begotten. The Holy Ghost is of the Father, and the Son:
not made, nor created, nor begotten, but proceeding.

So there is one Father, not three fathers,
One Son, not three sons,
One Holy Ghost, not three holy ghosts.

In this Trinity nothing is before or after, nothing is greater
or less: but all three Persons coeternal together and equal.

And so in all things, as has been said, the unity in
Trinity, and Trinity in unity is to be worshiped.

He, therefore, that will be saved, thus must think of the
Trinity.

But it is also necessary for eternal salvation that he also
believe faithfully the Incarnation of our Lord Jesus Christ.

For the right faith is that we believe and confess that our
Lord Jesus Christ, the Son of God, is God and man:
God of the substance of his Father, begotten before all ages:
man of the substance of his mother, born in the world.
Perfect God and perfect man:
Of a reasonable soul and human flesh subsisting:
Equal to his Father, as touching his Godhead:
Less than the Father, as touching his manhood:
Who, although he be God and man, yet he is not two
          but one Christ.
One, not by the conversion of the Godhead into flesh, but
by the taking of the manhood into God. One altogether,
not by confusion of substance, but by unity of Person.

For as the reasonable soul and flesh is one man: so God and man is one Christ:

Who suffered for our salvation:
Who descended into hell:
Who rose again the third day from the dead:
He ascended into Heaven:
He sitteth at the right hand of God the Father Almighty:
Thence he shall come to judge the living and the dead:
At whose coming all men shall rise with their bodies:
And give an account, each of his own works:—
Those who have done good shall go into everlasting life:
Those who have done evil, into everlasting fire.

—This is the Catholic faith, which, except every man believe faithfully and firmly, he cannot be saved.

> *Glory be to the Father,*
> *And to the Son,*
> *And to the Holy Spirit.*
> *Amen.*

SAINT ATHANASIUS

WE praise him as without beginning, because of him who has a beginning.
And adore him as everlasting, because of him who in time has come to be.
He that is without beginning made the Son a beginning of things originated; and advanced him as a Son to himself by adoption.
He has nothing proper to God in proper subsistence.
For he is not equal, no, nor one in essence with him.
Wise is God, for he is the teacher of wisdom.

ARIUS

O blessed one,
to thee I turn my gaze again.
Thou art my strength,
the Lord of all,
the Unbegotten,
the Beginning
and the Father of the Beginning,
who is the immortal Son.
Thou art the Great Light sprung from similar light,
circling in a manner that is ineffable from One to One.
O Son of God,
Wisdom,
King,
Word,
Truth,
Image of the Archetype,
Nature equal to the begetter,
Shepherd,
Lamb,
Victim,
God,
Man,
Highpriest;
and Spirit proceeding from the Father,
Light of my mind,
who comest to the pure and makest God of man,
look down in mercy.
As the years run their course,
grant that I may here and hereafter
be mingled with the whole divinity.
With hymns unending may I celebrate thee in joy.

SAINT GREGORY NAZIANZUS

RISING at dawn I give thee my promise, my God,
No deed of darkness or shame to allow or to do;
But, as lies in me, to yield thee today in its wholeness,
Remaining unshaken and lord of my passions for thee.
If ever I fall into sin, I disgrace the gray head of my
 priesthood
And the table I stand by to serve thee with gifts of thine
 own.
This is my purpose, O Christ, who art mine; O prosper
 my effort.

       SAINT GREGORY NAZIANZUS

O Word of our God, I betrayed thee, the Truth, with my
 falsehood,
When I promised to hallow the hours that vanish away;
In o'ertaking me night does not find me undarkened by sin.
I did indeed pray, and I thought to stand blameless at eve,
But someway and somewhere my feet have stumbled and
 fallen;
For a storm-cloud swoopt on me, envious lest I be saved.
Kindle for me thy light, O Christ, with thy presence
 restored.

       SAINT GREGORY NAZIANZUS

O Christ, I have lost the day that is past through the
    darkness of sin;
A storm of wrath surprised me and swept me away with its
    gust.
Grant that today may be pure and dowered with light.
Gregory, look to thyself: remember, thou look'st upon
    God;
Thou hast sworn: take thought that salvation be thine.

SAINT GREGORY NAZIANZUS

O all-transcendent God
    (what other name describes you?)
what words can sing your praises?
    No word at all denotes you.
What mind can probe your secret?
    No mind at all can grasp you,
Alone beyond the power of speech,
    all men can speak of springs from you;
alone beyond the power of thought,
    all men can think of stems from you.
All things proclaim you—
    things that can speak, things that cannot.
All things revere you—
    things that have reason, things that have none.
The whole world's longing
    and pain mingle about you.
All things breathe you a prayer,
    a silent hymn of your own composing.
All that exists you uphold,
    all things in concert move to your orders.
You are the end of all that is,
    you are one, you are all;

you are none of the things that are,
　you are not a part and not the whole.
All names are at your disposal;
　how shall I name you, the only unnameable?
What mind's affinities with heaven
　can pierce the veils above the clouds?
Mercy, all-transcendent God
　(what other name describes you?)

SAINT GREGORY NAZIANZUS

NOW do we give you our praise,
Christ to us, to God Word,
Light from eternal Light,
Dispenser of the Spirit's graces.
Now do we bless you, threefold Light
with the one brightness.
You it was who dissolved the darkness
and put the light there:
Light there should be for creating,
for staying the fluid matter
and shaping the world
and making its present beauty.
You it is who give men the light
of reason and wisdom,
give them an image
of the splendor above, the brilliance below;
that with the light that is theirs
they may see the light that is not theirs,
and all may be light.

You brightened the heavens
with their various stars.
You bade night and day
succeed each other peaceably;
the law you gave them was the law
of brotherhood and friendship.
At night after their labors
you give rest to our bodies—
our bodies born to much toil.
By day you spur us on to work
and do what pleases you,
that shunning the dark
we may hasten on to that day
which no sad night shall overwhelm.

With lightest of fingers
may sleep caress my eyelids,
that so my tongue may not for long
Be idle in its praise of you,
your creature cease for long
to hymn you with the angels.
Holy be my thoughts, be my thoughts in your presence,
as I lie down to rest.
Far from my mind this night
be the deeds that have sullied the day,
far from my dreams
the night's disturbing illusion.
Though my lips may not speak to you, God,
my mind must pursue you,
Father, Son, and Holy Spirit.
Honor, glory, power to you
now and in every age. Amen.

SAINT GREGORY NAZIANZUS

O Lord of Knowledge, who givest Wisdom, who layest
bare that which is hid in darkness, who givest speech to
those who proclaim glad tidings in thy great Power, who,
of thy goodness, didst call Paul, a persecutor for the time,
to become of thee a chosen vessel; who was pleased to
make him, then, to be called an apostle, and to be a
preacher of the Gospel of thy Kingdom:

O Christ our God, thou, even thou, art now the one God
and lover of men: We pray thee to grant us and thy whole
people a mind free from care, a clear understanding, that
we may know and understand what profit there is in that
holy teaching of thine, which now is being delivered unto
us, and how far it resembles thee, O Prince of Life! So also
make us worthy to be like unto it in every work, and in
faith, and to glorify thy holy name and to rejoice in thy
cross.

O Lord our God, who through thy holy apostles, didst
reveal the mystery of the glorious Gospel of thy Christ, and
didst, according to the immeasurable great gift of thy grace,
endow them that they might preach among all nations the
unsearchable riches of thy mercy: We pray thee, O our
Lord: Make us worthy of their portion and of their lot.
Grant us grace at all times to follow in their steps, that we
be like them in their conflict, that we behave like them in
the persecutions they, for Godliness, endured. Protect thy
holy Church, which thou didst found through them. Bless
the sheep of thy pasture: make this vineyard to grow,
which in Jesus Christ thy right hand has planted.

O Lord and master Jesus Christ, our God, who didst tell
thy holy apostles: "Many prophets and righteous men have
desired to see those things which ye see, and have not seen,
and hear those things which ye hear, and have not heard:
but blessed are your eyes, for they see, and your ears, for

they hear:" Make us worthy to hear and to do as thy holy Gospel teaches, through thy saints' supplications.

O thou who art long suffering, who art of great mercy and great truth: Take at our hands our prayers and supplications; place our cry, repentance, and our confession, upon thine unblemished altar in heaven! May we be worthy to hear thy holy Gospel, so to keep thy commandments, thy holy precepts, to yield from them fruit, a hundredfold, seventyfold, and fortyfold, through Jesus Christ our Lord.

Remember, O Lord, our fathers and our brethren who journey to foreign parts: bring them in peace and safety back to their home.

Remember, O Lord, the seed and the plants of the field: make them to grow, to multiply.

Vouchsafe, O Lord, the waters of the river and them bless.

Remember, O Lord, the airs of heaven; the fruits of the earth do bless.

Remember, O Lord, the safe preservation of both man and of his beasts.

Remember, O Lord, the preservation of this holy place, and of all places and monasteries of our orthodox fathers.

Remember, O Lord, thy servant, the ruler of the country.

Remember, O Lord, our fathers, our brethren, who are asleep, who rested in orthodox faith.

Remember, O Lord, those who have brought in to thee these gifts and those who parted with them, and those through whom the offering was made; give them reward which is from Heaven.

Remember, O Lord, those who are suffering affliction, who are in necessity.

Remember, O Lord, the catechumens of thy people: have mercy on them, confirm them in faith which is in thee. Cast out of their hearts remnants of every idolatrous worship, strengthen in their hearts thy law, thy fear, thy commandments, thy truth, thy holy precepts; grant them to know how to hold fast the words in which they have been instructed, so they be worthy of the washing of the new birth, for the remission of sins; make them temples of thy Holy Spirit.

O God, who in thy ineffable mercy didst send thine Only-begotten Son into the world that he should bring back to thee the sheep who were gone astray: We pray and beseech thy goodness, thy love for man: Blot out our sins, remit us our shortcomings, to the glory and honor of thy holy name, Father and Son and Holy Ghost, now and ever. We pray and entreat thy goodness, O thou lover of man!

Arise, O Lord God: Scatter abroad all thine enemies! Let all those who hate thy holy name flee from before thy face, and let thy people dwell with thy blessing, thousands of thousands, and ten thousands of ten thousands of years, to do thy holy will!

O great and eternal God, who didst create man for incorruptibility, who through the lifegiving appearing of thine Only-begotten Son, our Lord God, our Savior Jesus Christ, didst abolish the death brought in by the Devil's

hatred of man; who didst fill the earth with peace from
heaven, wherein the hosts of angels glorify thee, saying,
"Glory to God in the highest, and on earth peace to men of
goodwill:" Of thy goodwill, O God, fill our hearts with
thy peace. Cleanse us from all stain, cleanse us of all guile
and all infirmity, of all craft, all the remembrance of the
wickedness that puts on death: make us worthy, O Lord, to
greet one another with a holy kiss, that we may partake,
without condemnation, of thy immortal and heavenly gifts,
through Jesus Christ our Lord—

> Thou, who art Master, O Lord God of Truth,
> Who art from all eternity, who art forever king,
> Who dwellest in the Highest,
> Yet on the humble lookest down;
> Who didst create the heavens, earth, the sea,
> And all that is in it,
> O thou, Father of our Lord, and of our God
> And Savior Jesus Christ,
> Who didst create, through him,
> All things that are seen and not seen,
> Who sittest upon the throne of thy glory,
> Worshiped by all the holy powers,
> Before whom stand the angels,
> The archangels, powers, the authorities,
> The thrones, dominions, and the strengths,
> Around whom stand the cherubim full of eyes,
> The seraphim with six wings, with unceasing voices
> Praising thee, saying,
> "Holy! Holy! Holy are thou in very truth
> O Lord our God, Who didst form us,
> Who didst place us in the Paradise of joy!"

SAINT GREGORY NAZIANZUS

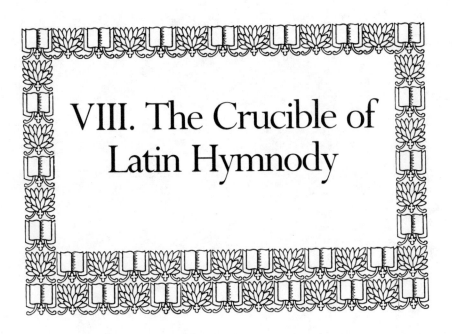

VIII. The Crucible of Latin Hymnody

Now let us sing in anthems sweet
To God the Father and the
Son,
Who with the Holy Paraclete
Forever reigneth, three in one.

SAINT AMBROSE

THE shortest bridge between early Christian hymnody and contemporary Christian worship is here. Not only have several of the hymns written by Hilary, Ambrose, and others been passed down from generation to generation and included in hymnbooks to this very day, but the now traditional hymn style, based upon quatrains and sung by the congregation, is here firmly established.

The Te Deum, with which we begin this selection of Latin hymns, derives from the Greek liturgy, another bridge. Attributed to Hilary, Ambrose, and even Augustine, this well-known hymn, or anthem, is more likely a composite of early Christian hymns from various sources.

The first extant Latin hymns were penned by Saint Hilary. His hymnbook is lost, and most of the hymns attributed to him are spurious. Those we have included are among the few deemed to be authentic. Studiously orthodox, Hilary introduces us to the strong trinitarian emphasis that distinguishes early Latin hymnody.

The reason for this stress on the trinity is matter for debate. Consider especially Hilary's "Ad Coeli Clara," where the Godhead consists of three inseparable and functionally complementary elements, underscoring the trinity as an image of balanced power.

One theory is that these hymns stem from the ongoing Christian polemic against pagan and Jewish critics, and also from the fourth-century theological controversies concerning the nature of the Godhead. Others suggest that the strong trinitarian emphasis suggests nothing more than the natural development of the trinity as a fit subject for worship and devotion. Whatever the source, this strong emphasis has influenced later hymnody profoundly.

Popular theology also continues to inform the hymnists. Most striking is the common motif of the sun, especially as a metaphor for Christ. This elaborates a recurrent theme in early Christian popular theology, also evinced by the image of Jesus as Helios driving the chariot of the sun in a Roman catacomb frescoe.

Briefly to introduce the hymnists in this chapter, Pope Damasus was the first to introduce rhyme to Christian hymnody, a practice universal today, but only apparently present in most other early hymnody, reflecting modern translations. Saint Ambrose, who so profoundly influenced Saint Augustine, did more than any other to establish Latin hymnody. Of hymns attributed to him, we only include those that have some claim to authenticity. Sedulius was a native of Ireland, later renowned in Rome for his literary accomplishments. Asterius, a bishop of Pontus, is little known, but his one extant hymn sings through the ages. Prudentius was a Spanish theologian and poet, perhaps the finest Christian poet of early centuries. He wrote several books of poetry, including the hymnal from which most of our selections are taken. We close with a selection of hymns from Fortunatus, a sixth-century Italian bard whose "Pange Lingua" and "Vexilla Regis" have long been acclaimed as two of the most beautiful Latin hymns.

O God, we praise you,
as Lord we confess you.
Eternal Father, all the earth reveres you.
The angels, the heavens and all the powers,
the cherubim and seraphim unceasingly proclaim:
Holy, holy, holy is the Lord God of hosts.
Heaven and earth are full
of your majesty and glory.
The apostles' glorious choir,
the prophets' eminent company,
the shining army of martyrs
praise you.

Holy Church throughout the world confesses
you the Father, infinite in majesty,
your true and only Son, the venerable,
the Spirit, too, who assists us.

You are a glorious King, O Christ,
the Father's eternal Son;
yet at your coming to take upon you
the human nature that you would release,
a virgin's womb had no dismay for you.
Drawing death's sting,
you opened the kingdom of heaven
to all who would believe.
You sit at God's right hand,

sharing the Father's glory;
and we believe that you will come and judge us.
We beg you, therefore, help your servants,
since you have redeemed them
with your precious blood.
With the saints be our lot
in eternal glory.

Save your people, Lord,
bless the race of your choice;
guide and support them always.
Day by day we bless you;
we will praise your name forever,
yes, forever.

Out of your goodness, Lord,
keep us from sin today.
Have mercy on us, Lord,
have mercy on us.
Lord, let your mercy rest on us,
for we put our trust in you.
In you, Lord, we place our confidence;
may we never be disappointed.

TE DEUM

THOU splendid giver of the light,
    By whose serene and lovely ray
Beyond the gloomy shades of night
    Is opened wide another day!

Thou true Light-bearer of the earth,
   Far more than he whose slender star,
Son of the morning, in its dearth
   Of radiance sheds its beams afar!

But clearer than the sun may shine,
   All light and day in thee I find,
To fill my night with glory fine
   And purify my inner mind.

Come near, thou maker of the world,
   Illustrious in thy Father's light,
From whose free grace if we were hurled,
   Body and soul were ruined quite.

Fill with thy Spirit every sense,
   That God's divine and gracious love
May drive Satanic temptings hence,
   And blight their falsehoods from above.

That in the acts of common toil
   Which life demands from us each day,
We may, without a stain or soil,
   Live in thy holy laws always.

Let chastity of mind prevail
   To conquer every fleshly lust;
And keep thy temple without fail,
   O Holy Ghost, from filth and dust.

This hope is in my praying heart—
   These are my vows which now I pray;
That this sweet light may not depart,
   But guide me purely through the day.

    "LUCIS LARGITOR SPLENDIDE," SAINT HILARY

THOU unbegotten God, the Sire,
    And thou, the sole-begotten Son,
Who, with the Spirit's sacred fire,
    Art everlasting, three in one;

To thee no mortal calls in vain,
    Nor doth the lover of the light
Lift up unheard a prayerful strain
    Nor blindly seek thy holy height.

Nay, Father, they that sigh for thee,
    And they that bow in humble prayer,
Or yield the heart on bended knee,
    Still meet the sweetness of thy care.

Reminded by the rising sun,
    To thee our grateful hearts we bring;
With love and praise and orison,
    In hymns and songs, we gladly sing.

Lord, let the day be one of light,
    Build all our labors unto thee;
Thou, who hast brought us out of night,
    Keep us in strong sincerity.

        "DEUS PATER INGENITE," SAINT HILARY

WHAT blessed joys are ours,
    When time renews our thought
Of that true Comforter
    On the disciples brought.

With light of quivering flame
   In fiery tongues he fell,
And hearts were warm with love
   And lips were quick to tell.

All tongues were loosened then,
   And fear, in men, awoke
Before that mighty power
   By which the Spirit spoke.

Achieved in mystic sign
   Has been that Paschal feast,
Whose sacred list of days
   The soul from sin released.

Thee then, O holiest Lord,
   We pray in humble guise
To give such heavenly gifts
   Before our later eyes.

Fill consecrated breasts
   With grace to keep thy ways;
Show us forgiveness now,
   And grant us quiet days.

"BEATA NOBIS GUADIA," SAINT HILARY

THE limit of the night is passed,
   The quiet hour of sleep has fled;
Far up the lance of dawn is cast;
   New light upon the heaven is spread.

But when this sparkle of the day
   Our eyes discern, then, Lord of light,
To thee our souls make haste to pray
   And offer all their wants aright.

O Holy spirit, by the deeds
   Of thine own light and charity,
Renew us through our earthly needs
   And cause us to be like to thee.

Grant this, O Father ever blessed;
   And Holy Son, our heavenly friend;
And Holy Ghost, thou comfort best!
   Now and until all time shall end.

"JAM META NOCTIS," SAINT HILARY

I am not worthy, Lord, mine eyes
To turn unto thy starry skies;
But bowed in sin, with moans and sighs,
   I beg thee, hear me.

My duty I have left undone,
Nor sought I crime or shame to shun,
My feet in sinful paths have run,
   Sweet Christ, be near me.

O, fill my soul with grief sincere
For mine offenses; let the tear
Moisten my pillow; Father hear,
   And grant repentance.

For all my many crimes, O Lord,
The pains of hell were just reward;
But thou, O God, my cry regard,
   And spare the sentence.

Redeemer, sole-begotten Son,
Father and Spirit, three in one,
Thou art my hope; as ages run
   Be thine all glory.

     "AD COELI CLARA," SAINT HILARY

FAIR as the morn in the deep blushing East,
Dawns the bright day of Saint Agatha's feast;
Christ who has borne her from labor to rest,
Crowns her as virgin and martyr most blest.

Noble by birth and of beautiful face,
Richer by far in her deeds and her grace,
Earth's fleeting honors and gains she despised,
God's holy will and commandments she prized.

Braver and nobler than merciless foes,
Willing her limbs to the scourge to expose;
Weakly she sank not by anguish oppressed,
When cruel torture destroyed her fair breast.

Then her dark dungeon was filled with delight,
Peter the shepherd refreshed her by night;
Forth to her tortures rejoicing she went,
Thanking her God for the trials he sent.

Barbarous pagans, escaping their doom,
Honor her virtues that brighten their gloom;
They whom the title of faith hath adorned,
Like her, earth's possessions and pleasures have scorned.

Radiant and glorious, a heavenly bride,
She to the Lord for the wretched hath cried;
So in her honor your praises employ,
That ye too may share in her triumph and joy.

Praise to the Father and praise to the Son,
Praise to the Spirit, the blest Three in One;
God of all might in Heaven's glory arrayed,
Praise for thy grace in thy servant displayed.

"MARTYRIS ECCE DIES AGATHAE," POPE DAMASUS

MAKER of all, the Lord,
    And ruler in the height,
Thy care doth robe the day in peace,
    Thou givest sleep by night.

Let rest refresh our limbs
    For toil, though wearied now,
And let our troubled minds be calm,
    And smooth the anxious brow.

We sing our thanks, for day
    Is gone and night appears;
Our vows and prayers in contrite hope
    Are lifted to thine ears.

To thee the deepest soul,
  To thee the tuneful voice,
To thee the chaste affections turn,
  In thee our minds rejoice.

That when black depths of gloom
  Have hid the day from sight,
Our faith may tread no darkening path,
  And night by faith be bright.

And let no slumber seize
  That mind which must not sleep,
Whose faith must keep its virtue fresh,
  Whose dreams may not be deep.

When sensual things are done
  Our loftiest thought is thine,
Nor fear of unseen enemies
  Can break such peace divine.

To Christ and to the Father now,
  And to the Spirit equally,
We pray for every favoring gift,
  One God supreme, a Trinity.

"DEUS CREATOR OMNIUM," SAINT AMBROSE

O radiance of the Father,
  Thyself our light and day,
We rise at night to praise thee,
  Assist us, Christ, we pray.

Drive from our souls all darkness,
   All thoughts and dreams of ill,
Be thou our guide and master,
   And be thy law our will.

Make strong thy faith within us,
   Thou knowest how weak we be;
Lord, hear in loving kindness
   The psalms we sing to thee.

All glory to the Father
   And sole-begotten Son,
And to the Holy Spirit,
   While endless ages run.

"CONSORS PATERNI LUMINIS," SAINT AMBROSE

WHILE morn awakes with wondrous light
   We come to thee, O Lord, in prayer;
Guard thou and guide our steps aright
   And keep us in thy holy care.

Lord, let our tongues be free from blame,
   Nor utter words of guilt or strife;
Lift up our eyes from deeds of shame,
   And all the vanities of life.

Our hearts be purged and purified
   That nought of evil shall remain;
From worldly vice and fleshly pride
   Our souls by temperance restrain.

So keep us, Lord, from evil free,
  Till fades in dusk the sunset flame,
That we unstained may come to thee
  And sing the glories of thy name.

All praise to God the Father be
  And to his sole-begotten Son,
And Holy Paraclete to thee,
  Now and while endless ages run.

"JAM LUCIS ORTO SIDERA," SAINT AMBROSE

THIS is the very day of God,
  Serene with holy light,
On which the pure atoning blood
  Has cleansed the world aright.

Restoring hope to lost mankind,
  Enlightening darkened eyes,
Relieving fear in us who find
  The thief in Paradise.

Who, changing swiftly cross for crown,
  By one brief glance of trust,
Beheld God's Kingdom shining down,
  And followed Christ the Just.

The very angels stand amazed,
  Beholding such a sight,
And such a trusting sinner raised
  To blessed life and light.

O mystery beyond our thought,
  To take earth's stain away,
And lift the burden sin hath brought,
  And cleanse this coarser clay.

What deed can more sublime appear?
  For sorrow seeks for grace,
And love releases mortal fear,
  And death renews the race.

Death seizes on the bitter barb,
  And binds herself thereto,
And life is clad in deathly garb,
  And life shall rise anew.

When death through earth has made her path,
  Then all the dead shall rise,
And death, consumed by heavenly wrath,
  In groans, and lonely, dies.

"HIC EST DIES VERUS DEI," SAINT AMBROSE

ETERNAL builder of the skies,
  Dread ruler of the night and day,
With glories thou hast blessed our eyes,
  To drive the stain of pride away.

To those that seem in gloom forlorn
  Thou art a light; our scattered fold
Now hear the herald of the morn,
  The splendor of its rays behold.

The day star rising from the wave
  Scatters the mist from heaven's blue,
And buried a sunless grave
  The dreams of error sink from view.

The sailors stand upon the deck,
  The sea grows mild, the waves subside,
The ship of evil lies awreck—
  Calm stands thy rock above the tide.

And hark the crowing of the cock!
  The sound shall rouse earth's erring sons;
Arise and seek the saving rock,
  Ye weary, weak and fainting ones.

Hope cometh with the morning song,
  The sick shall rise from bed of pain,
Ensheathed shall be the sword of wrong,
  And faith shall find her own again.

O Jesus guard thy wandering sheep
  From thy sweet fold ne'er more to stray;
Our feeble steps from danger keep,
  And fear shall melt in tears away.

Shine on our souls, O Living Light;
  From stain of error keep us free;
Let songs of praise by day and night,
  And vows of love arise to thee.

Now let us sing in anthems sweet
  To God the Father and the Son,
Who with the Holy Paraclete
  Forever reigneth, three in one.

"AETERNO RERUM CONDITOR," SAINT AMBROSE

O blessed light, the Trinity,
  In unity of primal love—
Now that the burning sun has gone,
  Our hearts illumine from above.

Thee, in the morn with songs of praise,
  Thee, at the evening time, we seek;
Thee, through all ages we adore,
  And, suppliant of thy love, we speak.

To God the Father be the praise,
  And to his sole-begotten Son,
And to the Blessed Comforter,
  Both now and while all time shall run.

"O LUX BEATA TRINITAS," SAINT AMBROSE

GOD of creation, wondrous might,
  Eternal power that all adore,
Thou rulest the changing day and night,
  Thyself unchanging evermore.

Pour light upon our fading day,
  So in our lives no dusk shall be,
So death shall bring us to the ray
  Of heavenly glory, Lord, with thee.

Father of mercy, unto thee
  We lift our voice in prayer and praise,
And to the Son and Spirit be
  Like glory to the end of days.

"RERUM DEUS TENAX VIGOR," SAINT AMBROSE

O splendor of the Father's face,
  Bringer of glory from above,
True light, and Fount of every grace,
  Illume our day with faith and love.

Pour on our way, O Sun Divine,
  Thy holy truth with rays serene,
And let the heavenly spirit shine
  With purging fires to make us clean.

The glory of the Sire we seek,
  The Father of enduring grace;
Lift up our spirits, fallen and weak,
  And guide us to thy dwelling place.

Confirm us in thy love divine,
  Smooth for our feet life's rugged way;
Our wills make ever one with thine,
  Lest evil lead our steps astray.

Be with us still as guard and guide,
  Keep us in holy chastity,
Let our firm faith on thee abide,
  From fraud and error hold us free.

Dear Christ, be still our drink and food,
  Our hope, our love, our lasting faith;
And be our souls each day renewed,
  Fired by the Spirit's quickening breath.

Thus joyful let the day go by;
  Our modesty like morn shall glow;
Our faith be like the midday sky,
  Nor gloom of doubt nor shadow know.

Lo, as the dawn brings forth the light,
   The Virgin brings the birth divine,
True God the Son in love and might,
   True God the Sire, in power benign.

To God the Father glory be,
   The same unto the sole-born Son,
And Holy Paraclete to thee,
   Now and while endless ages run.

"SPLENDOR PATERNAE GLORIAE," SAINT AMBROSE

FROM where the sun awakes the morn
   Unto his utmost westering,
We sing the Christ, the Virgin-born,
   The Prince of heaven and earth we sing.

Behold, the God of ages comes
   And taketh flesh of humble clay;
Man's Maker man's poor form assumes
   To wash the stains of flesh away.

A virgin's womb becomes the shrine
   That holds the Lord of heaven and earth,
Through stainless maid, by grace divine,
   The God-child hath his wondrous birth.

Her modest breast is made his home,
   The temple of her God is she;
Enshrined in Mary's spotless womb,
   He comes the world from doom to free.

He comes upon this happy morn,
   Announced by angel's heralding,
Known by the Baptist, yet unborn,
   Adoring in the womb his King.

On lowly bed of hay he lies,
   His palace but a stable poor;
The God that rules the earth and skies
   Doth all our wants and woes endure.

The angel choirs rejoice on high,
   Through radiant skies their voices ring,
The shepherds see the blazing sky,
   And bow before the Infant King.

All praise and power and glory be
   To Jesus whom the Virgin bore;
Father, be equal meed to thee
   And to the Spirit evermore.

        "A SOLIS ORTUS CARDINE," SEDULIUS

WHY fear the coming of the king,
   O cruel Herod? Christ, the Son
Asks nought of earth, but comes to bring
   To all who seek, a heavenly throne.

The Magi follow through the night
   The mystic star that goes before;
By light, they seek the Lord of Light,
   The King and God whom they adore.

Oh, purer than the morning ray,
 Celestial Lamb, thou comest to bear
Our sins, and wash our guilt away,
 That we with thee, God's love may share.

O Fount of Love! O power divine!
 We bow before thy holy might;
Thy word makes water pour as wine;
 Thy love brings day unto our night.

Jesus to thee be glory meet,
 Who shinest o'er earth in light and love,
So to the Sire and Paraclete
 Let earth resound and heaven above.

"CREDELIS HERODES DEUM," SEDULIUS

O night that is brighter than day,
O night more dazzling than the sun,
O night more sparkling than the snow,
O night more brilliant than our lamps!

O night that is sweeter than paradise,
O night delivered from darkness,
O night that dispels sleep,
O night that makes us keep vigil with the angels,

O night terrible for the demons,
O night desired by all the year,
O night that leads the bridal Church to her Spouse,
O night that is mother to those enlightened!

O night in which the Devil,
sleeping, was despoiled,
O night in which the Heir
brings the coheirs to their heritage!

ASTERIUS OF PONTUS

SERVANT of God, remember
The stream thy soul bedewing,
The grace that came upon thee
Anointing and renewing.

When kindly slumber calls thee,
Upon thy bed reclining,
Trace thou the Cross of Jesus,
Thy heart and forehead signing.

The Cross dissolves the darkness,
And drives away temptation;
It calms the wavering spirit
By quiet consecration.

Begone, begone, the terrors
Of vague and formless dreaming;
Begone, thou fell deceiver,
With all thy boasted scheming.

Begone, thou crooked serpent,
Who, twisting and pursuing,
By fraud and lie preparest
The simple soul's undoing;

Tremble, for Christ is near us,
Depart, for here he dwelleth,
And this, the Sign thou knowest,
Thy strong battalions quelleth.

Then while the weary body
Its rest in sleep is nearing,
The heart will muse in silence
On Christ and his appearing.

To God, eternal Father,
To Christ, our King, be glory,
And to the Holy Spirit,
In never-ending story.

                                PRUDENTIUS

GOOD captain, maker of the light
Who dost divide the day and night,
The sun is drowned beneath the sea,
Chaos is on us, horribly.
O Christ, give back to faithful souls the light!

                                PRUDENTIUS

LO the golden light appears,
  Lo the darkness pales away
Which has plunged us long in fears,
  Wandering in a devious way.

Now the light brings peace at last,
  Holds us purely as its own;
All our doubts aside are cast,
  And we speak with holy tone.

So may all the day run on
  Free from sin of hand or tongue,
And our very glances shun
  Every form and shape of wrong.

High above us One is set
  All our days to know and mark,
And our acts he watches yet
  From the dawning to the dark.

"LUX ECCE SURGIT AUREA," PRUDENTIUS

THE clouds, the shadows, and the night
  Long held in gloom both earth and sky,
Light enters, and the heavens grow bright,
  Christ comes, and lo, the shadows fly.

The blinding fog is pierced amain,
  By shining arrows of the sun,
Earth's golden rays return again,
  The glory of the morn is won.

The light is thine, O Christ! we see
  Thy glory in the open day;
With tears and songs we come to thee;
  Lift up and guide our souls, we pray.

Cleanse us from stain of sinful pride,
   And warm us in thy living light;
Thou art our heavenly lamp, our guide;
   Shine in thy sweetness, clear and bright.

To God the Father, glory be,
   And equal glory to the Son,
The same, O Paraclete, to thee,
   Forever reigning, three in one.

"NOX ET TENEBRAE ET NUBILAE," PRUDENTIUS

THE bird that heralds in the day
   Sings out his knell of passing night,
And Christ, whose love is still our stay,
   Recalls our souls to love and light.

He speaketh, "Leave your beds in haste,
   No more in ease and sloth abide,
Be sober, righteous, just and chaste,
   And watch, for I am at your side."

We call thee, Lord, in psalm and song,
   With prayers and tears we come to thee;
Lord, let our hearts be pure and strong,
   From sin and sorrow make us free.

Dispel the cloud of idle sleep,
   And break the bands that hold the night,
Our souls from stain of evil keep,
   And grant us, Lord, thy holy light.

To God the Father glory be,
   The same to Christ, the sole-born Son,
And Holy Ghost eternally,
   One God, one praise as ages run.

            "ALES DICI NUNTIUS," PRUDENTIUS

A sacred town is Bethlehem,
   Its walls are wondrous fair;
For Jesus, our salvation, came
   And made his birthplace there.

The star that leads the sages three
   Is bright as early day,
And in its light their God they see
   Enrobed in mortal clay.

They bow to earth as they behold,
   And Orient offerings bring,
The myrrh, the frankincense, the gold,
   As God, as man, as king.

Unto the King the golden hoard,
   As tribute they prefer;
The incense to the deathless Lord,
   To mortal man the myrrh.

To thee, O Christ, be glory meet;
   Thy name all lands adore;
Unto the Sire and Paraclete
   Like glory evermore.

      "O SOLA MAGNARUM URBIUM," PRUDENTIUS

O thou who seek'st the Christ to find,
    Uplift thine eyes on high;
For lo! to every humble mind
    His glory fills the sky.

His mighty wonders there behold,
    In boundless fields of light,
Sublime, eternal, and as old
    As heaven and ancient night.

Here is the nation's King indeed,
    Here Israel's mighty Lord,
To Abraham promised and his seed,
    Forevermore adored.

To him each prophet witnesseth,
    By word and sign sincere;
Acknowledged by the Sire, who saith,
    "Behold, believe and hear!"

To Jesus, who his light displays
    To babes, all glory be,
To Sire and Spirit equal praise
    For all eternity.

"QUICUMQUE CHRISTUM QUAERITIS," PRUDENTIUS

FRAME, my tongue, a song of wonder,
    Let the noble numbers ring;
Sing the glorious triumph crowning
    Our Redeemer, Christ the King;
Sing the sacred immolation
    That from death revoked the sting.

By the tree the crime of Adam
　　Plunged the earth in blighting sin;
From the tree man's woe was measured,
　　All the evil lay therein;
On the tree, by God's appointment,
　　Christ must die the world to win.

Thus the work of our salvation
　　Was by law divine ordained,
Thus by good to ill opposing,
　　Was the tempter's power restrained;
Whence the evil, thence the healing,
　　Whence came death true life is gained.

In his holy hour the Savior
　　From the halls of heaven is come,
Takes the flesh of human nature;
　　So to save the flesh from doom;
Born as man, the world's Creator
　　Issues from a virgin's womb.

In a stable poor and lowly,
　　He, a tender child is born,
With a manger for a cradle,
　　Our Redeemer lies forlorn;
Swathing him in bands, the mother
　　Shields the Babe from shame and scorn.

Thirty years are soon completed,
　　And the day of woe is nigh;
Comes the hour of man's redemption,
　　When the Christ is doomed to die;
On the cross, a lamb, uplifted,
　　Lo! the Lord of earth and sky!

With a crown of thorns they crown him,
   And they nail him to the wood,
With a lance they pierce his body
   Whence the water and the blood
Flow, till ocean, earth and heaven
   Bathe in the redeeming flood.

Faithful cross, a tree so noble
   Never grew in grove or wood;
Never leaf or blossom flourished
   Fair as on thy branches glowed;
Sweet the wood and sweet the iron
   Bearing up so dear a load.

Ah! relax thy native rigor,
   Bend thy branches, lofty tree!
Melt, O wood, in tender mercy!
   Christ, the King of Glory, see!
Veiled in human sin and sorrow,
   Slain, from sin the world to free.

Thou alone art found all worthy
   Earth's dread sacrifice to bear;
Thus to save the world from ruin,
   And the way to heaven prepare;
By his sacred blood anointed,
   Thou, O Tree, art wondrous fair.

Everlasting praise and glory
   To the blessed trinity;
Glory to the heavenly Father,
   To the Son like glory be;
Glory to the Holy Spirit,
   God eternal, one in three.

          "PANGE LINGUA," FORTUNATUS

THE royal banners forward fly;
The cross upon them cheers the sky;
That cross whereon our Maker hung,
In human form, by anguish wrung.

For he was wounded bitterly
By that dread spear-thrust on the tree,
And there, to set us free from guilt,
His very life in blood he spilt.

Accomplished now is what was told
By David in his psalm of old,
Who saith, "The heathen world shall see
God as their King upon the tree."

O tree, renowned and shining high,
Thy crimson is a royal dye!
Elect from such a worthy root
To bear those holy limbs, thy fruit.

Blessed upon whose branches then
Hung the great gift of God to men;
Whose price, of human life and breath,
Redeemed us from the thrall of death.

Thy bark exhales a perfume sweet
With which no nectar may compete;
And, joyful in thine ample fruit,
A noble triumph crowns thy root.

Hail, altar! and thou, Victim, hail!
Thy glorious passion shall not fail;
Whereby our life no death might lack,
And life from death be rendered back.

O Cross, our only hope, all hail!
In this time when woes assail.
To all the pious grant thy grace,
And all the sinners' sins efface!

"VEXILLA REGIS," FORTUNATUS

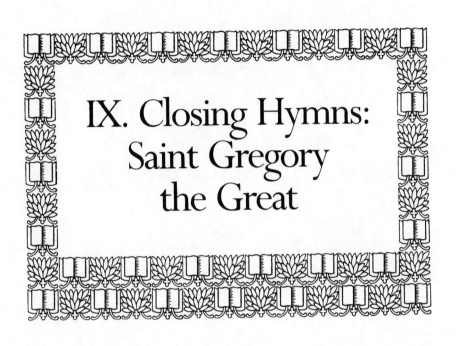

IX. Closing Hymns:
Saint Gregory
the Great

Let us join our songs with the choirs supernal,
In unending praise to the King of mercy,
So our souls may come to the halls of splendor
  Shining eternal.

NOCTE SURGENTES

L AST of the four great fathers of the Church, and founder of the medieval papacy, Saint Gregory the Great ushered the Church into a new age. He was selected pope in 590, before which time he had alternatively served as a papal envoy and as a monastic. Saint Gregory did not welcome moving from the monastic life, with its alternating rhythms of prayer, a common worship, work, and study, to the holy see, but he proved a masterful administrator during his fourteen years as pope. He was also a prolific and thoughtful writer. His most famous work, *The Pastoral Rule,* had a profound impact on the Church for centuries.

Most of the liturgical works attributed to Saint Gregory, including the Gregorian Chant and much of the Gregorian Sacramentary, are of later provenance, as are almost all the hymns which have been passed down through the centuries under his name. A handful of Saint Gregory's hymns have survived, however, and with these—each a jewel of mature, Christian hymnody—we shall close.

A number of important trends, noted in emergent forms in the earlier chapters, coalesce here. Forceful naturalistic imagery is harnessed by a meditative quietude. Earthly and divine spheres are melded through music into a joint enterprise. Hymns are salvific in bringing human souls into the divine presence, while their author is penitent and emphatic concerning the sole efficacy of divine mercy. There is consistent attention to the Trinity, and the hymns are used unequivocally to reinforce credal formulations.

But, above all, each of these jewels bears the characteristically bold imprint of its crafter: intensely personal, profoundly pragmatic: hymns of a savior of the Church.

RISE we, now, ere dawn, and begin our watching,
Lift our hearts in psalms, and in meditation;
And with voices tuned to the Lord, in music
  Sing his sweet anthems.

Let us join our songs with the choirs supernal,
In unending praise to the King of mercy,
So our souls may come to the halls of splendor
  Shining eternal.

Be thou blessed, O God, in thy might tremendous,
Spirit, Sire and Son, thou art God eternal,
One forevermore; let thy praise and glory
  Sound through the ages.

NOCTE SURGENTES

LO, now the shadows of the night
Are passing by; the changing light
  Purples the skies of morn; and we
  Our suppliant voices lift to thee
In prayer and song, O God of might!

Let all thy mercies, Lord, increase
Upon our erring hearts; surcease
   Of sorrow bring; and make us free
   From sin and shame and misery,
And grant us everlasting peace.

Unto the Father glory raise
With love and joy, in hymns of praise;
   So to the sole-begotten Son,
   And Holy Spirit, three in one,
Resounding to the end of days.

ECCE JAM NOCTIS

BENIGN Creator of the spheres!
Hear thou the prayers, behold the tears,
That in this holy season we
With Lenten fastings, pour to thee.

Searcher of hearts, we seek thy throne,
Man's feeble will to thee is known.
We bow in grief and pardon crave,
From error, Lord, thy suppliants save.

Much have we sinned in deed and word,
We bare our hearts before thee, Lord;
Thy tender clemency we seek,
Oh heal our wounded souls and weak.

Grant that we may the body cleanse
Of sinful stain through abstinence,
May lift our fasting hearts to thee,
From all defiling evils free.

O tender Godhead, three in one!
Be ours the will all crime to shun,
To know and keep thy laws divine,
And be the fruits of fasting thine.

AUDI, BENIGNE CONDITOR

DIVINE creator of the light,
  Who, bringing forth the golden ray,
Didst join the morning with the night
  And call the blessed union day;

We bow to thee, whose mighty word
  Made time begin and heaven move;
Hear thou our tearful prayer, O Lord,
  And warm us with the light of love.

Lord, let no crime our souls oppress,
  Or keep us from thy law divine;
Oh guard us by thy saving grace
  And make our wills accord with thine.

Still may we seek thy heavenly seat,
  And strive eternal life to gain;
Oh, keep us in thy mercy sweet,
  And cleanse our souls from earthly stain.

LUCIS CREATOR OPTIME

DEVOTIONAL AND TOPICAL INDEX

Benedictus, 6

Blessing, 7, 8, 13, 16, 102

Bride/Bridegroom, 88–92, 100–102, 141, 142, 145, 146, 147, 168

Charity, 10

Christmas, 6–7, 113–14, 210–12, 217

Church, 74–75, 92–93, 195

Cosmogony, 125, 130–34

Cosmos and Nature, 7, 14, 15, 19, 20, 21, 22, 42, 43, 47, 48, 49–51, 52–53, 54–55, 83, 84, 108, 113, 114, 145–47

Creed, 178–81

Cross, 108–109, 205–206, 213–14, 221, 222

Dance, 117–19

Death, 91, 148–49, 150–53, 205–206

Disease, 91

Easter, 65–67, 67–69, 153–57

Evening, 183, 186, 200–201, 202–203, 204, 212, 213, 214, 226

Faith, 10, 53, 92, 141–47, 148

Gloria, 7, 62, 110, 116, 117, 119, 217, 220

Grace, 53, 110, 116, 117, 118, 119

Homily on the Pasch, 70–83

Hope, 10, 53, 55

Hosanna, 7, 8, 135, 195

Hymn of John, 8, 9

Hymn of the Pearl, 102–108

Judgment, 23–26, 72–73, 75–76

Lamentation, 111–12

Lent, 227

Litany, 173–76

Logos, 8, 9, 37, 44, 45, 47–48, 64, 70–72, 108, 116

Magnificat, 5
Mary, 5, 168–73, 177–78
Midday, 208–10
Morning, 167, 183, 184, 196–97, 198, 199–200, 204–205, 214, 215, 216, 226
Mystery, 73–74, 108, 128–29, 184–85

New Year Hymn, 86–87
Nunc Dimittis, 7

Openness to God, 39, 40, 41–43, 45, 52–53, 85, 99, 100, 141

Patience, 92
Peace, 92
Pentecost, 198–99
Petition, 187–90, 214
Praise, 5, 8, 16, 18, 19, 27, 38, 51, 55, 62, 63, 83–84, 102, 108, 110, 112, 116, 147–50, 182, 184–85, 186
Profession of Faith, 12, 14, 15, 16, 17, 18, 20–21, 61, 64, 65, 82, 126

Protection by God, 64, 65, 66

Redemption, 6, 7, 10, 13, 17, 23, 55, 76–78, 80–81, 113, 114, 115, 130–34, 218–20
Reliance on God, 17, 28, 33, 34, 36, 46, 148, 206–207, 227–28

Satan, 150–53
Saint Agatha, 201–202
Suffering, 91, 109–10
Suffering of Christ, 78–79, 80
Sun, 86–87, 143–45

Te Deum, 195–96
Thanksgiving, 20, 51, 102, 126
Tribulation, 157–61
Trust in God, 64

Unity, 92

Witness to God, 34, 35, 36, 127, 128–29
Womb, 111
Wonder of God, 34, 35, 36, 47, 62–63
Worship, 20, 22

SOURCE AND NAME INDEX

A Solis Ortus Cardine, 210–11
Acts of Andrew, 108–109
Acts of John, 116–19
Acts of Peter, 109–10
Acts of Thomas, 99–108
Ad Coeli Clara, 200–201
Aeterno Rerum Conditor, 206–207
Ales Dici Nuntius, 216–17
Apostolic Constitutions, 62
Arius, 181
Asterius of Pontus, 212–13
Audi, Benigne Conditor, 227
Ausonius, 86–87

Beata Nobis Guadia, 198–99
Benedictus, 6
Berlin Papyrus, 63, 64
Book of Revelation, 19, 20, 21, 22, 28

Christian Sibyllines, 114–15
Clement of Alexandria, 83–85
Consors Paterni Luminis, 203–204
Corpus Hermeticum, 135

Credelis Herodes Deum, 211–12

Deus Creator Omnium, 202–203
Deus Pater Ingenite, 198
Discourse on the Eighth and Ninth, 126

Easter Hymn, 65–67, 67–69
Ecce Jam Noctis, 226
Ephesians Nineteen, 114
Epistle of James, 17
Epistle of Titus, 18
Epistle to the Colossians, 14
Epistle to the Corinthians, 10, 11, 12
Epistle to the Ephesians, 14, 15
Epistle to the Hebrews, 15
Epistle to the Philippians, 10
Epistle to the Romans, 12, 13

First Apocalypse of James, 126
First Epistle of Peter, 16, 17, 18

First Epistle of Timothy, 18
First Stele of Seth, 130–31
Fortunatus, 218–22
Foyyum Papyrus, 64

Gloria in Excelsis, 62
Gloria of the Angels, 6–7
Gospel of Bartholomew,
    110–11
Gospel of John, 8, 9
Gospel of Luke, 5, 6, 7
Gospel of Mani, 116
Gospel of Mark, 8
Gospel of Matthew, 8

Harp of the Spirit, 137–61
Hic Est Dies Verus Dei,
    205–206
Hippolytus, 65–67, 67–69
Homily on the Pasch, 70–83
Hymn of John, 8, 9
Hymn of the Pearl, 102–108
Hymn of the Resurrection,
    Two, 153–57
Hymns for a Time of
    Tribulation, 157–61
Hymns on Faith, Fourteen,
    141–42; Seventy-three,
    143–45; Eighty-two, 145–47

Ignatius of Antioch, 61, 114

Jam Lucis Orto Sidera,
    204–205
Jam Meta Noctis, 199–200

Lucis Creator Optime, 227–28
Lucis Largitor Splendide,
    196–97

Lux Ecce Surgit Aurea,
    214–15

Magnificat, 5
Martyris Ecce Dies Agathae,
    201–202
Melito of Sardis, 70–83
Methodius of Olympus, 88–92

Nisibene Hymns, Fifty,
    147–50
Nocte Surgentes, 226
Nox Et Tenebrae Et Nubilae,
    215–16
Nunc Dimittis, 7

O Lux Beata Trinitas, 208
O Sola Magnarum Urbium,
    217
Odes of Solomon
    One, 33
    Three, 33, 34
    Six, 34–36
    Seven, 36–38
    Eight, 39–41
    Eleven, 41–43
    Twelve, 44–45
    Thirteen, 45
    Fourteen, 46
    Sixteen, 47–48
    Twenty-three, 49–51
    Twenty-six, 51–52
    Thirty, 52–53
    Thirty-four, 53
    Thirty-nine, 54–55
    Forty, 55
Oxyrhynchus Papyrus, 62–63

Pange Lingua, 218–20

Proevangelium of James,
110–11
Pope Damasus, 202
Prudentius, 213–18
Psalm of the Naassenes, 125
Pseudo-Clementines, 112–13

Quicumque Christum
Quaeritis, 218

Rerum Deus Tenax Vigor,
208

Saint Ambrose, 202–10
Saint Athanasius, 178–81
Saint Basil, 168–73
Saint Cyril of Alexandria,
177–78
Saint Ephrem, 137–61
Saint Gregory Nazianzus,
182–90
Saint Gregory the Great,
223–28

Saint Hilary, 196–201
Saint John Chrysostom,
168–76
Second Apocalypse of James,
127
Second Stele of Seth, 131–33
Sedulius, 210–12
Solomon, Odes of. *See* Odes
of Solomon
Splendor Paternae Gloriae,
209–10
Synesius, 167

Te Deum, 195–96
Testament of Our Lord Jesus
Christ, 92–93
Third Stele of Seth, 133–35
Tripartite Tractate, 128–29

Vexilla Regis, 221–22
Vienna Papyrus, 64, 65

F. FORRESTER CHURCH is Senior Minister of All Souls Unitarian Church in New York City. Editor of Macmillan's *The Essential Tillich*, co-editor (with Terrence Mulry) of *The Macmillan Book of Earliest Christian Prayers*, and author of *Father & Son, The Devil & Dr. Church, Entertaining Angels, The Seven Deadly Virtures*, and *Everyday Miracles*, he also writes a weekly column for *The Chicago Tribune* on "Fundamentals." Dr. Church received his Ph.D. in 1978 from Harvard University in the field of Early Church History.

TERRENCE J. MULRY received his B.A. in Religion and master's degree in International Affairs from Columbia University, after which he worked for ten years in publishing. He is co-editor (with Dr. Church) of *The Macmillan Book of Earliest Christian Prayers*. Mr. Mulry is in his third year of the Master of Divinity program at Harvard Divinity School.